Death on the Doorstep
& other stories

Death on the Doorstep & other stories

A trial lawyer's memoir

Edward Z. Menkin

DEDICATION

To HGM and WJB, my mentors, who taught me
to be a better lawyer and a better man.

But it's the truth, even if it didn't happen.
Ken Kesey

Table of Contents

ACKNOWLEDGMENTS

I could not have written this book without the gracious support and assistance of many people. I would like to especially thank and recognize the Hon. Stephen J. Dougherty and the Hon. Joseph E. Fahey (ret), and the Office of the Onondaga County District Attorney, especially ADAs Rob Moran and Jim Maxwell, for their help in obtaining records of closed cases. I wish to also thank my honorary office assistant Mary DiMiero for her tolerance and good cheer and for always being able to solve one of my software problems. I also owe a debt of gratitude to Larry Fox, Esq., working lawyer, playwright, humorist, and Yukon real estate magnate, for his generous guidance and encouragement.

To my loving wife Laurie, I owe a debt of gratitude which I can never repay. Without her I would have had no career to speak of or write about.

A special thanks to Bob Gates, my editor, cheerleader, friend of 50 years, teacher, and photographer extraordinaire. Without Bob this project would not have come to fruition.

Finally, I wish to thank all my clients, those trusting souls who have blessed me with their confidence and allowed me the honor of navigating their stormy seas. Without them, I would have no stories to tell.

PROLOGUE

The stories in this book are all true. They happened to real people, some of whom experienced life-changing problems and all of whom for better or worse found their way to my door. I have changed but a few names, in deference to either privacy or propriety, and compressed a timeline or two for the sake of narrative ease. I will be ever grateful to these clients for entrusting me with the responsibility of steering their ferry across the River Styx.

I often wonder if I've made a difference. I don't mean have I made a difference in the lives of the people I've represented. The circumstances they found themselves in (a good part of which was their own doing) surely shaped their lives and their futures. For better, worse, or not so good, I know that I've made some difference. But it was only some. I'd be hard pressed to think of a single person whose life changed 180 degrees just because I stepped into it.

No, the bigger question has less to do with any difference I may have made in the lives of my clients and more to do with whether I made any difference in my community by representing them. It's more of a Big Picture issue: are we better off? It's not enough of an answer for me to repeat the conventional wisdom that if we're going to have justice, meaningful and fair justice, somebody's got to step up and act as a defender. A defender of what?

Just off the top of my head, and not in any particular order of their notoriety or the scale of their transgressions, here's a compressed inventory of some of the people and problems I've been involved with:

- a guy who illegally sold eagle feathers at a swap meet;
- a bank teller who helped herself to a slew of unauthorized withdrawals;
- a young guy being chased by a teenage mob turns and fires one shot at his pursuers, killing the kid in the lead – directly in front of the courthouse;
- a "financial advisor" who drained a series of retirement funds;
- a naive Jamaican teenager who assisted in moving tons of marijuana and AR-15s;
- a cop who spent his on-duty break time burglarizing the businesses he was patrolling;
- a guy who beat his girlfriend to death and then abducted their 5-year-old son who witnessed it, and then killed him too;
- a guy who suffocated his infant children for insurance money.

Do I need to go on? But I did. This is just a narrow sample of what my professional day-to-day has been like for the past forty years. If there's a theme here, please drop me a postcard to let me know. As far as I can tell, the one constant has been the standing up and pushing back. Some people want to own up and admit their wrongdoing; others not so much. No matter what they've done, they deserve to be treated fairly.

And I guess that's what I was supposed to do: make sure they're treated fairly. But after a while, dear God, it simply wears you down.

I'd like to believe that I survived all of this, and maybe actually thrived at it, because I'm smart, industrious, hardworking, and a believer in "justice" (no matter how you define it). But if I'm being totally honest, what kept my engine going and powering me through the human quagmire of the American criminal justice system was the combination of the drama and the challenge. And, even if it's somewhat embarrassing to admit, it was just plain fun.

What goes on in a criminal courtroom is the greatest free show in town. And for a pretty long time, I've had a front row seat.

IN PRAISE OF EGOTISM

L et me get this out front and out of the way. I'm in love with myself. Always have been. Always will be. No reason not to be. I had loving parents and a very happy childhood. My genes have blessed me with good health and I'm probably not quite as good looking as I think I am but I'm still more than OK with the morning mirror. I'm a smart charming guy and people tend to like me.

I'm an egotist and I know it. It doesn't bother me one whit that some people criticize me for this. Like Dizzy Dean once famously said, "If you can do it, it ain't braggin'." Well, I can do it and even my bitterest and most envious critics (are there really any actually left out there?) have to admit, I can do it. Did it, done it. OK, out of the way. Sort of.

I bring this up for a very particular reason. Once I started thinking about writing some kind of memoir, the inevitable product of advancing age, a declining number of clients who've decided they absolutely need Ed Menkin, an increasing number of people suggesting I ought to start writing a memoir, maybe because they got tired of hearing my stories, I came to the profoundly obvious conclusion that this was going to be a series of stories about my favorite subject:

me, my adventures, and my opinions.

Well, that's what a "memoir" is supposed to be, right? That started me thinking about the limits, the uses, and the nature of egotism because I certainly have a terminal dose of it. It set me to wondering if it's a bad thing at all.

I decided that it's not. In fact, having an ego and positive sense of yourself doesn't just have some very definite advantages in my line of work. It's essential. A client who's looking at the destruction of his life, his family, and his liberty because the dark forces of the State are bearing down on him at warp speed, does not want a lawyer who's afraid of stepping up, sticking his chest out, and telling the prosecutor to back the fuck off. That's not a mission for the weak of heart and you don't just need to believe in your client and his cause. You need to believe in yourself.

The danger, the place you can't go, is putting yourself, your interests, your love of being center stage, ahead of and in place of the client. I frequently tell clients, "It may be your bus, but I'm drivin'." To a large extent, that's true. But it's still their bus and you are the one trying to keep it from plunging off into a ravine. You are his samurai, his shield, his weapon to push back and if you don't believe in yourself in a major way your client's not going to believe in you either. So being an egotist with a proper purpose isn't something I'll apologize for. That's just how it is.

THE OPENING ACT: A SHOTGUN START

I t's one of the tritest lines in every prosecutor's opening statement that the opening is designed to be "like the table of contents of a book" so that the jury can get a preview of what is to come. This is both bullshit and pointless. First of all, like almost everyone else in Google America, jurors don't read books anymore. And if they do, they usually turn first to skim the pictures and then turn to the index to see if their names are there or if anyone they know is mentioned. If there are references to any kind of sexual performance or perversion, they go to those pages first. If the prosecutor is smart and knows what they are doing, the D.A. will present a compelling version of The Big Picture, laying out the story – and it's got to be a story – in such a way that the jury is left glaring at the defendant even though they are told by the judge and the prosecutor that they haven't heard any proof yet.

Of course, that's not how the law is supposed to work. The law says that the prosecutor is simply to inform the jury what the allegations are and how the case will be proven through the calling of witnesses and the presentation of evidence. No arguments allowed, no sales pitch, nothing to move the jurors permanently over to the D.A.'s side of the courtroom. Some prosecutors follow these proscriptions and forgo the opportunity to close the deal on the opening gambit. These types end up as in-house counsel to insurance companies or doing house closings for the rest of their career.

I'm not advocating breaking any rules here and, truly, any D.A. who breaks the rules deserves criticism. But you're not a trial lawyer if you're not an advocate, a zealous one, and if your cause is righteous, your cause deserves all you've got in your persuasion toolbox.

The defense opening has a different objective. If you stand in front of a jury and remind them that the burden of proof is always on the prosecutor and you and your client don't have to prove anything at all, you would then appear to be either a moron or a hypocrite if you go on to tell them what you're going to prove (one of my standby lines – which now sounds silly to me but I use it all the time – is that we could be sitting there playing pinochle and not ask any questions and the burden would still be on the prosecutor).

If the jury is sitting there, just having had the prosecutor barrage them with all the reasons your mope of a client is so profoundly guilty that a child could see it, you have to respond with something. They expect you to prove something, even though the judge – and even you – has just reminded them that you don't have to and you're not expected to. But something.

Forget the "table of contents" bullshit. Tell them a story. It's sort of the same story the D.A. is trying to tell – sort of – but it has a different point of view and you are definitely working towards a very different ending. One of the things I frequently do at these moments is that I hold up my hand with my fingers splayed out, wait a beat, and ask the jury, "Do you see my hand?" Since you're not allowed to engage them in conversation (wouldn't that be a hoot if you could do that during a trial?), I wait a second to let the question register and say, "No. You don't see my hand. What you see is the front of my hand. There's another side." And then I slowly rotate my hand so they can see the back. "Would you remember that? There's another side? Don't let this prosecutor show you only his side of this story. There's another side." I don't, of course, tell them either what that other side is or whether or not I'm going to "prove" it (or anything).

I'm just asking them to hold off judgment and be alert to "another side." I've done this so often that I'm nearly embarrassed to do it because it smacks of being one of those dreaded "lawyer's tricks" and something just short of phony; but I'm not embarrassed because it actually is effective and I've had more than one juror tell me he remembered it.

So, really, for both sides of the case, the opening statement is an important opportunity for each lawyer and how they go about it tells you a lot about where they are coming from and definitely where they are going.

My all-time favorite opening statement got me in trouble.

I was a young D.A., prosecuting a guy named Larry Williams, a genuine O.G. long before Snoop ever came up with the term. Larry was charged with Criminal Possession of a Weapon in the 2nd Degree, in this case a sawed-off shotgun.

Legally, it was a really interesting case because when Larry was stopped by the police (who had responded to a drive-by shooting minutes earlier), he was sitting in the passenger seat of a Pontiac Bonneville and under his seat were three separate things: the barrel of a sawed off shotgun, a stock, and a live slug. Under the law, Larry could only be convicted if he possessed a loaded operable firearm of a size which was "concealable upon the person" (i.e., a sawed-off).

His lawyer made the superficially logical argument that Larry was only a passenger, he didn't "possess" anything, and even if he was in proximity to the barrel, the stock, and the slug, those three things were not a gun. They were just three things. Not a gun. Made perfect logical sense. But, as most people know, logical sense frequently bears no relationship to legal sense. Larry's lawyer's argument was the equivalent of arguing against the law of gravity.

I countered with my legal version of the Ali Shuffle, dazzling the judge with cases and statutes (all written or decided, of course, by judges and lawyers who used to be prosecutors) which held – as a matter of law – that everyone in a car is presumed to possess whatever is in the car (unless they rat out the true possessor);

and not only that!, if the components of a firearm are in close proximity and can be readily assembled, then those components are a gun;

and not only that!, if the "operable firearm" is in proximity to live ammunition, the quickly assembled components not only constitute an operable firearm they constitute a loaded firearm;

and not only that!, but once the barrel was attached to the stock, the whole thing was under 27" thereby meeting the "concealable upon the person" requirement and qualifying the possessor thereof to a lengthy stay in a State-run facility with three hots and a cot for a very, very long time.

I got the barrel and the stock from the evidence vault and practiced assembling them quickly. Very quickly. It got to the point that I could actually do it blindfolded and I was stunned at how easy it was to assemble and disassemble these two things.

My cop friends pulled my coat on the subject of street guns like this one. The whole point of the detachable barrel is to get your shots off and start booking, tossing the barrel in one direction, the stock in the other, making it harder for the police to find anything. Apparently, Larry hadn't gotten the Memo containing this particular gem of street wisdom because the stock and the barrel were laying together on the Bonneville carpeting under his seat. Maybe he was saving them for his next school project, I don't know.

But even though nobody could finger him for the drive-by, he was still sitting atop of what I was going to show was a loaded sawed-off, no matter how many pieces it was in.

Larry's lawyer brought a motion to suppress the gun on the basis that the police had no cause to stop the car. Denied. He then brings a motion to rule that the gun was not a sawed-off, "concealable upon the person." Judge rules this is a fact for the jury to decide so the motion is denied.

We pick a jury and as luck would have it I couldn't have ordered a more perfect group for this case if Amazon was conducting a one-day flash sale of "12 Citizens Likely To Convict Someone of a Gun Crime." All men. All with military experience. 10 of them owned shotguns. Guaranteed to be diddling with the stock and the barrel as soon as those pieces of evidence went into the jury room.

You may be wondering why Larry went to trial in the first place and didn't try to save himself some prison time by plea bargaining. As I said before, Larry was hard-core O.G. but that wasn't the only reason we're going to trial over the sawed-off. For Larry, this was a pure two-fer.

While this case was pending, Larry got indicted for murdering a guy named Raymond Ford whom he shot five times in the back. At close range. In a bar. In front of 10 witnesses. Larry might have thought that he was Michael Corleone at Louis's Restaurant in the Bronx when he shoots Sollozzo and McClusky and nobody can or will identify him. Three of the witnesses are Raymond Ford's cousins and they already hated Larry for an earlier street beef. Larry's not going anywhere. He would just as soon spend a few days in court on the gun trial as wander around the day room in the Justice Center looking for a pickup b-ball game or playing hearts. Larry knew he was going down on the Raymond Ford homicide and he didn't give a shit. I knew he was going down too, but I did give a shit. He wasn't getting a freebie off me.

So now it's time for my opening statement. I'm usually not a suit and tie kind of guy, but part of the standard trial package is conveying an aura of seriousness of purpose so when I'm on trial I usually dress like I'm attending a rich client's kid's bar mitzvah. Not this time. I dug out a brown baggy three-piece corduroy ensemble which I apparently thought looked very cool when I was a graduate student and tried it on in my office in view of a full-length mirror. This was not my customary daily exercise at self-admiration. I assembled the shotgun, slid the stock deep into the generous right front pocket of the baggy suit, and then nestled the barrel along my right side up to my armpit. The folds of the brown corduroy were indistinguishable from the deadly verticality of what once was Larry's gun. Perfect. I then took the gun out, gathered it up with the rest of my trial file, photos, and evidence and headed over to the courtroom.

There's always a few minutes at the start of each trial day when there's a lot of milling about, setting up, and sphincter tightening. I take advantage of the distractions by ducking into a small bathroom conveniently located inside the courtroom. (They don't make courthouses now like they used to. You need to take a pee, you need three forms of I.D. and a card pass to get into the bathroom down the hall.) I then slide the gun into my pocket and up my side and walk stiffly out the door, reminding myself it wouldn't be a good idea to sit down.

The Judge enters and everybody is told to "Please rise." Not a problem, 'cause I'm still standing. As is his habit, Judge Burke says, "The People are here, the Defendant and his counsel are here. We'll have your opening statement Mr. Menkin."

I really can't remember much about what I mostly said in my opening statement. I was still very much a rookie prosecutor and I probably gave them the "table of contents" bullshit. But I do remember I'm giving them the story of the drive-by, the stop, the separate pieces of weaponry on the floor of the Bonneville under Larry's seat, and then, when I'm winding down, I get to the issue of concealability:

Now one of the issues we're going to deal with is whether the gun in question is something that is concealable upon the person. The Judge is going to instruct you on what the law says about that. Now, I've been talking to you here for about 10 minutes and I doubt that any of you realize that I'm armed.

And with that, I slowly draw out the sawed-off from under

my coat.

Pandemonium. One of the jurors gapes open-mouthed and slightly rises from his chair. Larry's attorney is decompensating, shouting for a mistrial. I hear Larry say – clearly – "Man, that was slicker than snot." Judge Burke is not amused. He sends the jury out, listens to the mistrial motion, thinks about it, and denies the motion, telling me that if I was intending to do something like that I should have given him some prior notice. But since, as I argued, the gun was coming into evidence anyway, he couldn't find anything legally wrong. He wags his finger at me, "No more heroics."

Well, Larry was right. It was slicker than snot. Apparently, however, my snot was a little too slick for the Appellate Division which, woefully lacking a sense of the dramatic or even a sense of humor, reversed the conviction that I had persuaded the jury to come back with.. I still say it was the greatest opening statement I ever gave.

DEATH ON THE DOORSTEP

PART I: City Man in the Morning Paper

Serious trouble has a way of finding me. I don't send drummers and hawkers out to the town square to bring it my way. And I don't pay some production company to shoot a lawyer cartoon for television luring the felony-stricken to my door. ("Call the Law Office of Ed Menkin Where Your First Felony Is Free!") It just shows up. People call me. Other lawyers call me. That's usually how it happens. I'm not an aloof kind of guy. Far from it. But I don't do a walk-in business and to get to see me so I can consider whether I can or want to help you usually requires at least a call or maybe an e-mail.

But there was this one time. I went looking for trouble. And I found it

The Sunday paper lay fat and unread on the kitchen table. Actually reading it was quickly becoming a quaint custom, the internet being far more available (though hardly more reliable) and an endeavor which was mercifully without the coupons and comics. The latest update on the width of Kim Kardashian's rear end wasn't of much interest to me and whatever else passed for "news" between its pages wasn't holding much of my attention lately either. Still, as my wife is overly fond of pointing out, I am incapable of eating either breakfast or a casual lunch without having something to read in front of me and since the internet service at our lakefront cottage was down that morning I was left to wade through a half ream of colorful newsprint to find, one might laughingly call, the "Local News." At least, I thought, a nugget of genuine interest might have broken through overnight.

So, in the process of spooning my Frosted Flakes from bowl to mouth I spot a headline entitled "CITY MAN ARRAIGNED IN BIZARRE MURDER CASE." Let me translate part of this for you: in my community, as I'm guessing in many others, "City Man" means a black guy. The coupling of a brother and a homicide in one easy to read caption is, sadly, not uncommon. In fact, it's generally how it goes in most people's minds. It was the "Bizarre" part of the headline that drew my attention. What the hell was that about? Was there such a thing as an almost-murder? A semi-murder? A murder that's not really a murder? All murders are bizarre in their own way.

Murder and I have had more than just a passing acquaintance over the years. I've represented mob assassins, desperate husbands, crazed boyfriends, jilted lovers, and depraved fathers, all of whom somehow or another found a creative way to end someone else's life in their own customized fashion, usually for a reason that seemed pretty good enough to them at the time but looking back on it a reasonable person might seriously question their judgment on that score.

Murder, usually, is a one-off crime. The person committing it is typically someone who has steered clear of the law for most of their life except for this one teensy weensy misstep. And the ways of murder are as grotesquely varied as the human imagination can conjure up in its evil complexity: "Let me freshen that vodka tonic with another shot of antifreeze dear"; "I'll go tuck in the baby while you check to see that her life insurance policy is still current"; "You payin' for this ammunition?"

So it wasn't "City Man" or homicide that drew my attention to the story; it was the "bizarre" part. How strange does a murder have to be to win that label contest in the weekly campaign to sell newspapers? Well, as it turned out, pretty strange.

Here's the basic story as it first appeared: Jeff Peterson, a "City Man," is returning home at 4:30 in the morning with his wife after an all-night birthday party and breakfast with another couple at Denny's. They live in a corner house with a small side porch entrance. The wife is up on the porch inserting her key in the door and Peterson is two steps down. Not only is it dark at 4:30 A.M. but the corner streetlight is out. Suddenly, from out of the bushes rushes this guy, Shaheen Bean, another "City Man," wearing a hoodie, high on PCP, brandishing a 9 mm Ruger fully loaded with a clip of hollow point bullets. Mr. Bean's not selling subscriptions to Better Homes & Gardens. Apparently, Jeff Peterson's bravery countervails his fear and he lunges at the guy. They grapple. The wife is screaming. Two shots go off. They both go down. More grappling. Two more shots. The gunman catches one in the hip and another to the back of the head. He is quite dead. Shot with his own gun. Peterson tosses the gun into the street, sits down on the curb, and awaits the arrival of the police.

This is a murder? A guy and his wife are attacked by a gunman on the steps to their own home, the guy shoots the attacker to death with the attacker's own gun, and this constitutes a crime? I must have missed that extra credit class in law school which taught Advanced Prosecutorial Thinking.

When the shooting first happened, the police responded immediately of course but given the fuzzy circumstances of who did what to whom they didn't immediately arrest Jeffrey Peterson. They took him and his wife in for questioning, took their statements and photographed their condition, and then released him. They left it to the District Attorney and the Grand Jury to decide what to do and continued their investigation.

About a month later, the District Attorney Bill Fitzpatrick together with Chief of Police Frank Fowler, with a fresh indictment in hand, had gone all-channel press conference on what they now decided was an outrageous execution murder. They ominously pontificated on the limits of self-defense when guns are in the wrong hands. They didn't spend much time on the minor key subject of whose hands the gun started out in. But no matter.

Let me be honest here: by halfway through the news article I already yearned for this case. I'm a reasonably busy guy and I've certainly had my share, maybe even more than my share, of high-profile cases. Maybe because I can string at least two coherent sentences together in front of a camera, I've been accused of being a media hog. OK, I'd plead guilty to that if pressed to it. But even with the Frosted Flakes dissolving in my mouth I recognized this was the case I'd been waiting for my entire career, that rarest of a diminishing species: a winnable murder case. In the right hands – my hands.

There's only one roadblock to my grand plan for glory: Jeff Peterson already has a lawyer. Señor Sal.

Señor Sal

Jeff Peterson's choice of Sal was a good one. Sal was one of the smartest guys in his law school class and had plenty of what some might call "experience." Sal once had a Yellow Pages ad (when the Yellow Pages were around and useful) that read "Experience Like No Other." This was not hyperbole or puffery. Many lawyers had been prosecutors before they turned to defense work. Sal could check that box. A lucky few got to be part-time judges in Town Court, a nice steady gig to cover your office overhead (not to mention the added perk of grown adults addressing you as "Your Honor" all the time and some lawyers you really couldn't stand being forced to stand up when you come into Court). Sal had that covered too.

The piece that really set Sal apart from the herd was the Federal inmate entry on his resume. A couple of months at FC Allenwood for helping a client launder some cash gave Sal the chance to regale his homeys with how he learned to make grilled cheese sandwiches on the prison radiator and how to brew pruno by using apples, sugar, ketchup, and fruit cocktail. To hear Sal tell it, it was Jimmy Cagney rattling the tin cup against the bars of the Big House. But in reality it wasn't much more than a couple of months locked in a college dormitory with recovering alcoholics and balding accountants who had gotten a little too creative with their clients' money.

Sal was likeable and smart. He was, however, sometimes

deficient in the judgment part of the job. Early on in his practice, he parlayed a series of wins for a small parade of Dominican drug dealers so that each time the local narcs would pick up a suspect inconveniently laden with a little more cocaine than personal use would justify, the refrain would be "Tráeme al abogado drogo." "Get me the drug lawyer" may actually have been translated into several languages because one detective I knew swore to me he saw it written in Bosnian on a downtown bar men's room. When "El Abogado Drogo" got too hard to remember, it was replaced by the snappier honorific of "Señor Sal." It actually got to the point where a small group of CID drug detectives went to a local silk screen company and commissioned a handful of tee shirts emblazoned with " El Abogado Drogo" over a headshot of Sal. A collector's item for sure. If he could have gotten a few, Sal would have handed them out with his business cards.

Still and all, whatever his colorful deficiencies, Sal had real talent and was a good choice to represent Jeff Peterson. And because he was my friend, it never occurred to me to try and snatch the case out from under him. I was just plain envious. As a moth to flame, however, I was drawn to the drama and the possibility that I could get at least within shouting distance of the Jeff Peterson "murder" case. Finishing my light breakfast, I formulated a plan that was ingenious in its simplicity: Better Call Sal.

Happily, the conversation wasn't long. Sal answered his phone on the first ring and I bypassed the customary niceties.

"Oh, Sally, what a case."

"You want in? Would love to have you."

Not more than 15 minutes after I read about City Man's

dilemma, Jeff Peterson now had two lawyers. And I didn't ask for a fee.

Getting to Know Jeffrey Peterson

I have a lawyer friend who claims that anything more than the first fifteen minutes he spends with a client, any client, any problem, is a complete waste of time. OK, mister, I got it. Got your problem, got your story, let me handle it, I'll send you the bill.

That's not my usual m.o. Not at all. Maybe it's my compulsion to get to know people and to meld knowing them with feeling for them that drives me to spend a lot of time getting to know a client. It generally fuels my passion for the work and helps me focus. Sometimes though, that's led to sadness and disappointment, especially when my client-now-friend gets sent through that steel door at the side of the courtroom, not to return for seven, nine, or forever. But it's how I do and I'm comfortable with it.

With Jeff Peterson, it was a different story. Jeffrey had had, shall we say, a "colorful" life – fathering eight kids by a multitude of beautiful women, a handful of prior convictions including felony assault, robbery, weapon possession, and drugs. But in Jeff's case I was far less interested in his resume or the content of his character than in the idea that he was being unjustly prosecuted for defending himself.

Despite my lack of initial interest in Jeff's life story, there was no escaping the fact that his past was colliding with his present. Even if District Attorney Bill Fitzpatrick had been inclined to view Jeffrey's shooting Bean in the head as an act of dark and desperate heroism (which is how I saw it even if Fitz didn't), such marginally romantic notions were wiped away for the police and the D.A. by Jeffrey's rap sheet. The largest ink blot staining that inventory was Jeffrey's 1998 conviction for conspiracy and cocaine distribution that earned him a twenty year to life sentence. Ah, that would be life, as in you're not coming back here no more.

There were three things that bothered Fitz about all of this and drove his determination to prosecute Jeffrey as relentlessly as possible. Number one, the guy was a major drug dealer in the community. Number two, Jeffrey did not man up and cop a plea for a lesser sentence and had the unmitigated nerve to actually exercise his constitutional right to a trial. And finally – and this was the clincher for Fitz – as the result of the repeal of the Rockefeller drug laws by a bunch of panty-waisted New York City liberal state legislators, Jeffrey's so-called "life" sentence got reduced after he had done just seven years because of the "Rockefeller Drug Law Reform" laws and he walked out of prison on early parole after "only" twelve years. Not life, not 20. 12 years. There was little to nothing Fitz could do about the change in the sentencing laws, but he would be goddamned if he was going to pass up this chance – any chance – to change Jeffrey's housing accommodations and re-book him back into the crowbar hotel where Fitz thought he ought to be. So, for Fitz, shooting another guy in the head was a plenty good reason to charge Jeffrey Peterson with murder and not to even momentarily linger over the possibility that the shooting was justified. As far as Fitz was concerned, like The Dude in "The Big Lebowski" said, "This shall not stand."

Jeffrey's past loomed large as the main, perhaps only, reason that he was getting prosecuted. But it also was the main, and definitely only, reason the shooting happened in the first place. The thing that caused the drug-addled Mr. Bean to rush up to Jeffrey in the darkness with a gun in his hand had a whole lot to do with the fact that Jeffrey had just been released from prison.

To most people, making parole after twelve years would be a chance to start over, breathe some fresh air, go out for lunch, and try and avoid drug dealing. At least for a little while. It had only been three months since Jeffrey had gotten his freedom back, but as far as the players on the street were concerned, Jeffrey was heading back to the game. If not already in it. Whether that was true or not (and I can tell you with absolute confidence that I absolutely didn't know one way or the other), it didn't matter. Jeff Peterson was out. His street rep was such that to the average knockabout working the corner, he had to have had a stash in his house. Or, if not a kilo or two, at least a stack of that cash he must have put aside for that day when he didn't have to buy ramen noodles from the prison commissary any longer. So the real reason for Bean looming out of the darkness with his gun (and maybe his companion laying in the bushes yards away) was that this was a planned home invasion. Nothing personal against you and the old lady, Jeff. We're just gonna take your shit.

Whether Jeffrey was protecting his tainted assets was, for me, quite beside the point. Guy with a gun attacks you and your wife at your doorstep doesn't seem to me to be an opportune time to calmly discuss alternative resolutions. Jeffrey did what he had to do and I couldn't have cared less if there were other considerations from the past at play.

So, it was for this reason I didn't invest a whole lot of time on "getting to know" Jeff Peterson. It was the injustice of it that drew me in. An added bonus for me was the chance to once again go mano a mano with D.A. Bill Fitzpatrick, my career-long frenemy who had been huffing, puffing, and hyping the outrageousness of this street execution. It was with mild disappointment, then, that I learned he had assigned the case to Assistant D.A. Christine Garvey, one of his more senior trial lawyers.

The King of New York Passes

Stylish, witty, whip smart, and utterly devoted to doing the right thing – no, I'm not talking here about myself – my friend Langston McKinney was retiring from the City Court bench. Having labored in the trenches as a Legal Aid lawyer and then giving private practice a shot, Langston was elected as a City Court Judge and had earned both respect and deep affection from pretty much everyone who knew him. He was not just a hero to the African American community but someone who established himself early on as a judge who knew when to get an over-eager prosecutor to take his foot off the gas pedal of the Justice Express when common sense dictated an alternative resolution. Sometimes it took a little longer to get to the right place and Justice was not a hurried concept in Langston's courtroom. He may have been the snappiest dresser in town, but a watch was pretty much a superfluous accessory for him. He was late for everything. Including his retirement ceremony.

A big crowd had gathered in the large ceremonial courtroom of the old County Court Building and pretty much everyone who was someone in the law biz was milling about waiting for the program to begin. Everyone that is except Langston. Since this was to be expected, people used the time to meet, greet, be seen, and generally bullshit with each other.

I found myself next to Matt Driscoll, the handsome and affable Mayor of Syracuse, and we were engaged in a high-minded and substantive discussion congratulating ourselves over how lucky we were to have good looking wives. We were then joined by another guy with a good-looking wife, Bill Fitzpatrick, the District Attorney of Onondaga County, otherwise known to me as The King of New York.

I have a long history with Fitz. He is not so much a public official as a force of nature. We have had some titanic battles, dramatic confrontations somewhat akin to Ali-Frazier except that Joe Frazier won at least once. I have played some small part in burnishing his legend, providing the noble and sometimes fierce opposition to his cause which, according to him, is always righteous, never wrong, and deserving of resounding vindication.

When out of town lawyers contact me to ask what kind of guy he is, I invariably tell them that there are only two things you need to know about Fitz: his father was a cop and his brother a priest. (His mother of blessed memory also happened to be one of the wittiest people I've ever met). He has been the District Attorney so long that there is at least one full generation of once young lawyers who didn't know that there were DAs before him or that the public office he occupies will not be eliminated upon his death. He is probably the most talented trial lawyer I have ever faced and I've faced him plenty. Our friendship is strong enough that I am one of a very few people who can tell him to his face he is full of shit and I don't believe I am delusional in thinking he actually considers that possibility for more than a beat or two when it comes from me.

Probably because I am a member of The Big Boys Club,

Fitz delights in needling me whenever the opportunity arises. His motivation is not so much a mix of sarcasm and cruelty as it is his need to self-validate his Big Tuna status over another fish of nearly equal size swimming in the school.

So back to the crowd milling about waiting for Langston. Having exhausted the topic of good-looking wives, Mayor Matt asked me what I was currently working on. Before I had the chance to entertain Matt with the riveting story of the developing Jeffrey Peterson self-defense case, The King of New York seized the conversational initiative. "Hey, Matt, listen to this. Eddie thinks he's actually gonna get this guy off." What followed was of course his grotesquely embellished and skewed version of how a career drug dealer who some panty-waisted judge let out of prison early had cowardly executed the poor mope who knew where Jeff had stashed his drug kingdom proceeds and stupidly attempted to cross him. Shot him in the head point blank! Outfuckingrageous! Menkin thinks he's gonna get the guy off!

I waited for Fitz to finish fulminating, paused a beat, and, not merely for Matt's benefit, but mostly for my own, I said "Yeah? If it's such a fuckin' winner, how come you're not tryin' it?" At that moment, they announced from the podium that Langston had finally arrived and we should find our seats.

The Struggle for Discovery:

What Really Happened on Genesee and Ellis?

As I mentioned earlier, Fitz had assigned ADA Christine Garvey to the Peterson case. Christine, a slim dark-haired beauty, was someone I hadn't dealt with before. The story on the street relating to Christine was that she was a strong believer in the strength of her own trial skills and the depth of her judgment, a confidence supported by neither her trial skills nor her judgment.

The DA's Office purported to maintain a policy of "open file discovery," a high-minded sounding rule of fairness which basically said that every defendant would have ready and full disclosure of what evidence there was against him. Christine apparently didn't get the memo. She preferred the Kabuki theater version where you spelled out your request in writing and she responded by acting out a pantomime which was basically one step removed from Duck Goose. For instance, when we asked for police reports, Christine was happy to fire up her copying machine and crank out a full 98 pages, illuminating mostly for the liberally applied black magic marker redactions blotting out such irrelevancies as names and addresses of witnesses, the number and content of the torrent of 911 calls coming in after the flurry of gunshots neighbors heard or thought they heard at 4:30 in the morning, and the name of the 911 caller who not only witnessed the shooting from 75 feet away but recorded the last gunshot. She was offended and "personally insulted" when we actually complained about it to the judge. In bits, dribbles, and pieces, we haltingly got some "discovery."

What we discovered turned out to be at least as interesting and bizarre as the newspaper's first version of the case itself. It also became fairly obvious fairly quickly why Christine didn't seem to be a big fan of the open file discovery policy.

The D.A.'s version of what happened here wasn't too far off from Fitz's initial thumbnail rant to Matt Driscoll. Jeffrey Peterson had, in fact, once been a pretty big-time drug dealer, someone with the good looks, smarts, and courage to be the Syracuse version of Stringer Bell in "The Wire." Jeffrey's smarts, however, didn't succeed in keeping him out of prison and he wound up getting sentenced to something on the dark side of forever.

Take, for instance, the gunshots. Jeff said there were four. His wife said there were four. The police recovered four shell casings. Sounds like four, doesn't it? Well, for openers, only two bullets (the forensic types like to refer to these as "projectiles") were recovered, unfortunately located in Mr. Bean's hip and head. Since the bullets were hollow points, cruelly designed to shatter and explode upon impact, what we were left with were multiple fragments of these two projectiles, each cluster located in places which did not bode well for Mr. Bean's continued health and wellness.

Despite the fact that the police evidence technicians "processed" the scene and festooned the lawn and porch area with a small herd of numbered yellow plastic evidence markers (as if laying out a grid to connect the dots for a child's drawing), they couldn't and didn't discover any other "projectiles." This would not be all that great a mystery (maybe the other bullets flew up into the air?) except for the fact that we also eventually learned of a raft of 911 callers reporting that the corner of East Genesee and Ellis had gone all Baghdad at 4:30 in the morning and some frightened neighbors had reported as many as 4, 5, 7, 8, 10, and/or 12 shots fired.

Bearing in mind that a) the defense never has to prove anything, and b) confusion is always the defendant's friend, we didn't have to work very hard to come up with what has now become famously known as "alternative facts."

Alternative fact #1 – the old standby: the police did a shitty job investigating the scene. Always a favorite, so adaptable to nearly every single case. (You don't think O.J. got off because he was actually innocent do you?) Alternative fact #2 – the even older standby: the Plan B suspect.

Maybe there was another gunman. Maybe Mr. Bean had backup who lit up the scene with a few rounds of his own and then fled once he realized that Jeff Peterson was fighting back and things were going south. Sound farfetched? Think Sal and I cooked that one up just sitting around imaging ways to obstruct justice? Well despite Christine's parsimony in teaspooning out discovery, we learned enough to know that Mr. Bean almost certainly had a wing man, although what he may have been up to remained a little cloudy.

Still, we sure would've liked to find any of those "missing" bullets. Sure enough, there came a day when Jeff's father in law, a really fine guy who had the generosity to lease his well-maintained rental house to his daughter and Jeffrey at a pretty modest rent, noticed a small hole in the ceiling of the outside porch. A little probing with a flashlight and small pocketknife suggested to us that this was a bullet hole and that buried within was a previously unrecovered bullet. From Mr. Bean's gun? from the Plan B accomplice? Using a protractor and a long length of string convinced us that the point of origin was almost certainly at the location of Jeff grappling with Bean on the lawn adjacent to the porch.

We were liking this discovery big time as it supported a couple of important lines of defense: Standby Defense #1, that the police did a shitty job processing the scene (and never saw the hole or recovered the bullet); theory #2, that Jeffrey and Bean were on the ground when at least one shot was fired upwards; theory #3, "the grassy knoll defense" that there was an additional gunman.

Not to say that the Earth quivered beneath our feet when we came upon this development, but this was big for us.

So, here's this afternoon's pop quiz: what would you do in the circumstance? Remove the bullet? Sit on it? Get your own forensic guy to do a report? Kudos to Sal on this one: we called the police. Even though there was something elegantly counterintuitive about it since part of our defense was the SPD incompetently processed the scene, the evil genius simplicity of this solution was that it would have forced them to admit their own initial inadequacy while at the same time compelling them to do forensic testing and comparisons (remember that they already had Bean's gun, two bullets, and four shells) on their dime, not ours.

So I made a call to a friendly lieutenant ("friendly" being a relative term here since no copper really wants to be known as a homey of a defense attorney) and broke the good news/bad news of the stray bullet hole. He was actually inclined to do something about it immediately since he was one of only a handful in the department who didn't think charging Jeff Peterson with anything other than ridding the streets of a public menace was such a hot idea. Sure enough, a forensic crew went back over, poked around some, and then discovered and recovered the errant slug in the porch ceiling. It turned out to have been fired from Bean's gun.

Sounds like the right thing happened there, doesn't it? Well, not according to Christine. Within twenty minutes of me calling the cops, I get a blistering phone call from her, bleating on and on over how and where did I get the nerve to interfere with her investigation and where did I get the stones to give orders to her police officers? I was pretty proud of myself in restraining my instinct to tell her to fuck off. I responded in the most dignified and professional manner possible, by holding the receiver out about eighteen inches from my ear, saying nothing, and then just hanging up when she was done venting. Not in the finest tradition of the Bar, but it felt pretty good actually.

Although Christine's futile harangue was a memorable event for me, it turns out that there was a deep and fun back story playing out at the time, the details of which were completely unknown to me. Even though both Sal and I had long trafficked extensively in lawyer gossip, D.A. gossip, and police gossip, we were completely unaware of the active shooting war going on between the police and the D.A. over our very own case. It wasn't just that a couple of coppers had their doubts about whether this was a crime at all (and, to be sure, a significant majority of the department was solidly in favor of locking Jeffrey's ass up this time for good, but there were a few dissenters); it was more in the manner of a deep resentment over the D.A.'s office frequently outsourcing their forensics and not trusting the SPD lab guys to do what they thought they were pretty good at. Unbeknownst to us, this particular squabble was festering for quite some time and whether Christine had had a hand in stoking or quelling the dispute, I cannot say. What I can say and do know is that the main reason she was displeased over our call to the cops was that it showed that at least a few defense lawyers in town thought the SPD lab people competent enough to step in and address a ballistics problem, a backhanded endorsement that was sure to be brought up the next time the DA went out to hire an out of town suit.

This backchannel feud became clearer to me after two curious incidents, neither of which had anything to do with the brilliance of my own efforts on behalf of Jeffrey Peterson.

The first was a call out of the blue from a cop. Although he had previously earned a well-deserved place in my Witness Hall of Fame (he proved himself to be not only candid but reasonably helpful in a previous trial when I cross examined him), his call was not simply a matter of him liking me and just wanting to help me out in the Peterson case. No, it was because he wasn't just mad but rather seething over how the D.A.'s Office was treating the SPD forensic guys. So he offered to conduct his own private seminar for me on the unique features of the 9mm recovered from the scene.

He showed me how the round that had "stovepiped" in the chamber reasonably supported our theory that when Jeffrey was grappling on the ground with Bean he could have grabbed the pistol in such a way that Bean, not Jeffrey, had fired the bullet into his own head and Jeff's hand over the ejection slot had caused the next round in the gun to be jammed. (For those of you who maintain something less than lifetime membership in the NRA, stovepiping is a type of malfunction that occurs when a cartridge case is not ejected fully when a pistol is fired and the cartridge case is trapped in an upright position during its ejection.) I had previously known nothing, of course, of this ballistic mystery and was grateful for the education. And although I was wondering, at the time, why this copper was being so generous with his off-duty hours, I was not inclined to delve too deeply into the pedigree of his gift of arcane and useful knowledge.

Ordinarily, had I not had the minor distraction of preparing for a homicide trial, I would have more fully explored the unrest between the police and the D.A.'s office. Even though it would have made for prime coffee shop gossip, Sal and I had too much else to do to get ready. But the next time it rubbed up against the Peterson murder case, it was just too blatant to ignore. But that was later.

Plan B

Sal and I had always thought there was another gunman. Or at least that Bean had backup. After all, no matter how crazed and drug-addled a guy might be, what kind of nitwit charges at his targets, an unarmed couple, out of the bushes, from 50 feet away, and across the street without some sense that one of your homeys is also in the darkness and has your back?

This wasn't the grassy knoll in Dallas or the guy with the black umbrella gazing at JFK getting shot lunatic theory. We had reason to argue it. Despite the eyedropper doses of discovery we were getting from Christine, we slowly learned a set of factoids each of which standing alone didn't amount to much more than discordant stray notes played on a rusted harmonica, but when played in harmony they seemed to tinkle out a tune vaguely resembling reasonable doubt.

Take, for instance, the small twisted baggie of cocaine found up the street, a block west of the shooting. The residential area where the incident took place was mostly modest aging one family post-World War II houses, but it was not The Hood. You might find the occasional McDonald's wrapper tossed on a street corner, but an 8ball twisty of blow was definitely out of place, the kind of thing an accomplice would drop if he was booking from the scene. Far fetched? Not when you add it to the testimony of the father and son up the street who after being awakened by hearing several gunshots and looking out their window, saw a black male in a hoodie running west crossing the street where the baggie was found and then through their back yard. Right after the gunshots.

As James Bond himself once coolly observed, "Once is happenstance. Twice is coincidence. Three times, it's enemy action."

We didn't really expect the jury to start solving the mystery of the fleeing accomplice (although I've had trials where 12 people astoundingly obsessed on trivia that neither the judge nor the lawyers thought was even remotely relevant.) We didn't really expect to argue that the police "failure" to identify and run this phantom accomplice to ground was attributable to poor detective work. We didn't care who this guy was, what he was doing there, or whether he was Shaheen Bean's backup. He just was. Or could have been. That was the point.

Through the entire trial, we did all we could to get the jury to put themselves in Jeff Peterson's position and situation. How swift, frenzied, and violent were the moments of the crisis he was facing in his front yard? Did Bean have another weapon on him? Did he have backup? Someone else coming to kill him and his wife? It wasn't unreasonable for Jeffrey to be thinking those thoughts. And it wasn't unreasonable to argue that there was another gunman. Or could have been. That was the point. Taking Bean out in self-defense under those circumstances would not have been unreasonable.

If I had to bet money on it, I'd go with the accomplice being real. And I'd go with James Bond. It was enemy action.

The Castle Defense

Despite my admiration for Jeff Peterson's manly courage in reacting to the deadly peril facing him and his wife, and my instinctive belief that that alone would save him from a jury's condemnation, I also realized that the law puts limits on the use of self-defense and that Fitz's argument that Jeff had crossed a forbidden boundary when he shot Bean in the head after Bean was disabled by the hip shot at least had a basis in law. Despite the drama, we needed a legal defense. We had one.

Under the law in New York, and pretty much everywhere in all systems of justice, a person has the right to defend themselves. To be sure, there are variations of this commonsense notion (including the somewhat controversial "stand your ground law" in Florida) but the basic premise is that if someone is coming at you you have a right to repel them and defend yourself. Provocation has some influence in shading your right; for example, how far can you go if you are the initial aggressor? What if you are the one casting a racial slur and the offended party comes at you with a baseball bat? Can you pick up your own baseball bat? How about your gun? It depends on the totality of the circumstances.

The basic rule in most jurisdictions is that you can meet force with equal and proportional force. If a guy is threatening you with a baseball bat, you can use your own bat to defend yourself. But since a bat has a limited range of harm and can only inflict damage at close quarters, you can't just take out your gun and shoot him from 20 feet away. If you can safely retreat, you should. In fact, in some scenarios, bizarre as it seems, you have to retreat.

But all the rules change if you are in your house. New York follows the doctrine of "The Castle Defense," the theory that every person has an unfettered and absolute right to defend their home, their "castle." If you encounter a burglar in your house, you can shoot him dead. No questions asked. Doesn't matter if he's armed. You don't have to retreat. (Where would you retreat to anyway?)

Well, since we were going to be in a courtroom where the rules of law apply instead of sitting around a coffee shop debating if Jeff Peterson did the right thing, Sal and I had to break down the event to ensure Jeff's conduct complied with the rules of self-defense. There was no question that Jeff and his wife were assailed by deadly force (Bean's gun). So we could check the box that limited the response to "equal and proportional force" (Bean's gun, but this time in Jeff's hand). And we certainly didn't have to linger over the "duty to retreat." They were at their home.

The trickier part, and the place where we might be vulnerable, was the D.A.'s argument that Bean was disabled when Jeff shot him a second time and the threat had been dissipated. Our answer was The Castle Doctrine. When the attack started, Jeff was at the bottom of the porch steps. Is that "home"? Almost home? Near home? His wife had her key in the door. She was certainly "home." And no matter where he was physically situated, Jeff Peterson had an absolute right to use deadly force in defense of another who herself was unarmed and in or at "the Castle." Circuitous as it might first seem, two complementary theories of defense presented themselves: Jeff was entitled to defend himself with deadly force because being at the bottom of the porch stairs he was defending himself and his home; or Jeff was entitled to defend his wife with deadly force because she definitely was "in" her home .

Lawyers have a tendency to overthink these things. As will be seen, by the end of this saga none of this would matter very much. We had no way of knowing this, of course at this point in time, so we soldiered on with our trial preparation.

Timing in Death is Everything

It took a while, and a couple of subpoenas (which Christine reflexively but futilely opposed), but we eventually got the records of the Time Warner Security alarm system for the Peterson's home, the police scanner broadcasts, and the computerized data base for the 911 calls, most particularly the call made by Debbie Kinsey reporting the struggle on the lawn across the street in the darkness, her call actually recording the last shot. Because computerized technology is so precise, especially in cases recording emergency signals, we were able to identify the exact time of various events down to the tenths of a second.

This helped us understand not only the sequence of events as they were actually unfolding but, because it all unfolded so rapidly, it also reinforced our theory that we wanted the jury to understand that the attack and response were moments of real and very sudden crisis.

Our one "soft" data point was the time that Jeffrey's wife turned her key in the porch door lock. According to her, and to Jeff Peterson, Bean rushed at them just as that was happening. We didn't have an exact time for that. But what we did know was that the Time Warner Security home system was designed in such a way as to give the person making entry thirty seconds to deactivate the alarm from the panel in the interior of the home before the alarm siren went off and an emergency signal was transmitted.

Since the Time Warner Security alarm signal was received at 04:42.42 hours, that meant that the attack began at 04:42.12 hours. To be sure we were right about the 30 second alarm delay, I used my video camera to record Jeff's wife inserting her key into the door, turning it, entering the house, and approaching the interior alarm panel, all the while holding a stop watch in the foreground of the shot. As predicted and hoped for, the alarm went off after exactly 30 seconds.

So now we had a reliable starting point for the attack (04:42.12 hours). And no one listening to these calls or viewing a spreadsheet chart of their sequence and content could regard the attack on Jeff Peterson and his wife as anything other than a frenzied onslaught of bullets flying:

04:42.12	Door opens
04:42.32	1st 911 call ("multiple gunshots")
04:42.42	TW Alarm activated
04:42.44	2nd 911 call (Mrs. Kinsey)
04:42.45	3rd 911 call ("multiple gunshots" "7 or 8")
04:43.19	4th 911 call ("4 or 5 shots")
04:43.37	Gunshot heard on 2d 911 call (Mrs. Kinsey)
04:43.46	5th 911 call ("6 shots; people screaming")
04:44.33	6th 911 call ("multiple gunshots")

It wasn't lost on us (or the D.A.) that Mrs. Kinsey's call wasn't initiated until some 30 seconds had elapsed after the attack began and, further, by the time the "last" shot was fired and picked up on her cell phone (at 04:43.37), a previous 911 caller reported hearing "7 or 8" shots. Human fallibility being what it is, and given that people were excitedly reporting a traumatic event they are witnessing or hearing on a 911 call, still, couldn't a reasonable person conclude that there were multiple guns being fired at the scene? That there was more than one shooter? More and more, the prosecution theory of an "execution" was looking less and less probable. Plan B, the second shooter, was looming large for us, especially after we learned that Sgt. Todd Cramer, the first police officer who responded to the scene (04:46 AM) reported that he asked Jeff what had just happened and the response he got was "They attacked me."

Pan B was looking better.

Going from Wingman to Fearless Leader

We were four months into the Jeffrey Peterson case and still struggling with discovery and shaping our defense when Sal had engine trouble. And it was the kind that doesn't just cause you to pull over on the highway for a few minutes. It was more akin to your doctor calling you up to tell you your tests have come back and you have cancer. Sal had long lingered on the Feds to-do list, and they had now decided it was his time to get indicted.

The very short version of this saga is that a trio of bulk marijuana dealers claimed that Sal had helped them out by phonying up some paperwork to show their supplier that a 50 lb. load had been intercepted by the police (which, of course it wasn't. The phony paperwork was their way of stealing the load.). I pledged to help and defend Sal, but even he recognized that the Jeff Peterson case had to be a priority for me. So we put his troubles on a side shelf until we could resolve the shoot 'em up on Genesee and Ellis. Eight months later, it would a week-long trial in Federal Court and several years off Sal's life to bring about an acquittal for him. But to say his attention was distracted while we defended Jeff Peterson would be a minor understatement.

There's never a good time for this sort of thing to happen and of course the timing was particularly inauspicious for Jeff Peterson (not to mention Sal). So discretion dictated a reshuffling of tasks and responsibilities and a reversal of roles. I suddenly found myself pretty much in sole charge of the case, with Sal providing what wingman support he could. When thinking back to that first morning I learned about the prosecution of Jeffrey Peterson and feeling that I really wanted the case, I certainly didn't want it that badly. Sal was out, I'm in. Pretty much flying solo.

My preference has always been to try and solve problems myself. I like to make my own breakfast. I'm not ungrateful when my wife makes it for me; I just want it the way I want it and it generally saves both time and irritation if I get my Monk's Bread white toast the way I want it with just the right amount of butter on it. I'm neither selfish, nor unappreciative. It's just more satisfying if I do it myself. Same goes for my law practice. My judgment and experience tell me that a client in a criminal case prefers a lone samurai to a platoon of corporals. Sal's help had been enormously helpful up until the Federal Grand Jury's nastygram came along addressed to him.

So now it's me at the stick, Jeffrey in the cargo hold, and Sal trying to deal with a smoking engine in a Sopwith Camel way off in the distance.

The Right Judge for the Right Case

The Peterson case was assigned to the Hon. Joseph E. Fahey, Onondaga County Court Judge. Joe was a former defense lawyer with real skill, a genuinely witty guy, someone who was smart enough not to have an aversion to work while at the same time also smart enough not to work too hard unless he really had to.

Like most great trial lawyers, Joe was a great storyteller who, like me, was frequently his own best audience. He was one of several children of the late City Court Judge James Fahey and had inherited not only his father's modified work ethic but also his very dry sense of humor. A famous Jim Fahey line, which combined the weariness of being a City Court Judge with the insight that there are a ton of other things to do in life, was when he sustained an objection at trial "in the interests of brevity."

Many years before, I had tried a couple of cases with Joe as co-counsel when he was a defense attorney. It was a pleasure to work with someone who, like Rumpole, regarded a criminal trial as basically harmless fun (except for the part where sometimes your client gets convicted).

One time Joe and I were representing two jail deputies accused of tuning up an inmate who refused to obey an order to get out of his cell and then hurled his AIDS-laden feces onto my client's uniform and badge, a form of civil disobedience which my client did not appreciate. My guy and Joe's rather large client removed the inmate from his cell in a manner not exactly in conformity with the Sheriff's Manual (or the Geneva Convention for that matter). The entire episode was witnessed by about two dozen inmates who were milling about the cell block, each skell more eager than the next to put our guys' conduct in the worst possible light come trial time.

We're about to sum up and Joe was going first. I say to him, "Joe, what are you gonna tell them?" and he responds "I'm gonna tell them that if they convict our guys they might as well turn the jailhouse keys over to these lyin' scumbags." I say, "No, you're not really?" Joe says, "Watch me." He did. Our guys were acquitted.

Joe was the perfect draw for me. A good friend who was smart on the law, had no interest or even inclination in getting involved in the case or putting his thumb on the scales of justice, and was going to just leave me alone. I knew that he'd let me try my own case.

PART II: The Trial

Who Will Judge?

Showtime.

Is my self-defense justification gonna beat your twenty-five to life murder?

After six months of pretrial technicalities and procedures, the motions, the discovery and investigations, the subpoenas, the posturings and minor irritations, Jeff Peterson's trial would come down to a trial of just a few days. At least I thought it would only be a few days. On one level, I was looking forward to the drama and the challenge. But what continued to weigh heavily on my mind, as it had from the very start, was the moral question of what Jeffrey Peterson had done and whether a group of ordinary people would see it the way we saw it. Who could say that it really was wrong, no matter how it had unfolded? Could I get twelve people to see it that way? It all came down, as it always did, to a jury.

Picking a jury is one part art form, one part sales routine, and one part luck. Actually, forget the art form and the sales routine; even if you know what you are doing, it's mostly luck. You can go to all the seminars you want to or pay an outrageous amount of money to a "jury consultant" who dresses up his particular version of bullshit and voodoo as a valuable sociopsychological service, but if the stars aren't aligned for you with the right combination of 80 or so people in the room to start with, no amount of standing on your head or shamelessly congratulating a doddering WW II vet for his service is going to get you the "right" jury.

Jury selection in the Peterson trial started, as all of these felony matters do, with a pool of 100 or so citizens of the County supposedly chosen at random who were unlucky enough to be ambushed at their mailbox, finding a jury summons along with the latest issue of Consumer Reports, Pizza Hut coupons, and their utility bill.

They were first prepped downstairs in the Jury Assembly room with a gentle but patriotically stirring video piece of propaganda with celebrities telling them how important jury service is and what they can expect if they are chosen to sit. When Robert DeNiro or Tom Hanks tells you something like that, odds are you're going to take it at least half seriously. After all, they're on television. They must know what they're talking about.

So after the Commissioner of Jurors weeds out and excuses people who just can't do it this or next week ("I have a leg amputation scheduled for this Thursday," "We have prepaid nonrefundable tickets to the Wagner Festival in

Bayreuth that my husband Hans has been saving for for 10 years" "I have a neighborhood Bund meeting"), they are herded up into a somewhat smaller courtroom, our courtroom, and quietly fill the benches with the same blinking look of incomprehension of people who are returning to Earth after a series of alien abductions.

Judge Fahey then welcomed them all over again, informing them as to where they are (as if by now they don't know), what they are doing there (this in particular can remain a mystery well into the trial; some never do comprehend it), what the charges are (no need to be concerned; it's only a murder trial), and who the attorneys are and what their roles are.

Once this opening ceremony is completed, 12 or 14 or sometimes 21 jurors are called to the jury box and they are individually questioned by the Judge and then the lawyers. Judge Fahey first asked the prospective jurors to come up to the bench to quietly discuss either personal or sensitive matters that they would prefer not announcing to a roomful of strangers. This frequently happens. Jurors may not like being asked certain things in public: like, have you ever been arrested? whatever did happen to that sexual abuse charge your brother-in-law was facing? will your chronic incontinence problem distract your attention if you have to sit and listen to three hours of testimony?

And to make them particularly destabilized and uncomfortable, sometimes the defendant is standing right there in the clutch of quiet conversation. He has a right to be there, but I've generally discouraged my clients from bellying up to the bar and joining in the occasional jocularity. Jeff Peterson, in a shirt and tie, looking handsome and very much alone, didn't join us in these intimate conversations.

Voodoo and cynicism aside, picking the jury is a critical exercise. In the Peterson homicide case, it wasn't just important, it was the whole case. It didn't take long for the assembled jurors to get the thumbnail version of what happened. Jeffrey and his wife had been accosted by a gunman on the doorstep of their home in the darkness when they came home on a very early morning and after a frenzied struggle, Jeff, who was unarmed, shot the attacker to death with the guy's own gun. The DA was calling this a murder. They were going to sit in on a murder case. (Just like on T.V.!) If I wound up with some hyperanalytical University sociology professor who didn't like guns in anybody's hands or an overly inquisitive engineer whose social preferences ran to statisticians wearing pocket protectors, I was done for before we ever got to the minor issues of evidence and proof.

I wanted jurors of ample girth, comfortable shoes, a sense of humor, and teenage daughters at home. Most of all – and this is true in nearly every case I've ever tried– I wanted jurors who would listen to me. Not to the prosecutor. Not to the judge. To me. I want to have at least the twinkle of recognition in someone who could at least meet my eyes and nonverbally signal their openness to me selling them something. I couldn't care less what their specific answers were, what their favorite color was, what the last book they read was, if they voted every year or not. Doesn't matter. Only one test: will they listen to me?

And this benchmark has nothing to do with my love of being the center of all things. It has to do with counting on them still being with me at the end of the trial. If I can show them what I've got and how it's a far more reasonable version of reality than the one the prosecutor has been selling, I'm gonna win and my client gets to go home. No voodoo involved. Will this person listen to me? Are we connecting?

In the Jeffrey Peterson case I had a special reason to want to have these intimate confabs at the bench instead of out in the whole room. Given the story we were working with, it was an important and relevant fact that there was a Time Warner security system at the house and when Jeff's wife turned the key it activated the delayed alarm system, giving her exactly 30 seconds to get to the security panel to deactivate the alarm before an emergency signal went out to Time Warner. Because of the pandemonium ensuing just below the side porch during the attack, she never did deactivate the panel and the alarm was shrieking throughout most of the hurly burly.

That was important in the case because I not only had the exact time the alarm signal was received by Time Warner down to the hundredths of a second, but I also had the exact time of the neighbor's 911 call narrating the event and recording the last gunshot (and that too was down to the hundredths of a second). I wanted to be able to show the jury that the entire event – from opening the door to the attack to the last gunshot -- lasted exactly 87 seconds with bullets flying, not very much time to decide anything, much less make a decision to murder a guy, even a guy with very bad intentions.

Given the facts I had, I needed to identify jurors who would relate to protecting the security of their families and their homes.

My thinking was pretty much that no prospective juror was going to be comfortable with answering the question,

"Does your home have a security alarm system?" in front of 60+ strangers, some of who could easily be part-time burglars taking notes. It wasn't the only question being asked at the bench, but in my mind it was a pretty important one. And even without the invaluable assistance of a jury consultant to explain it to me, I figured out on my own that it also gave me a little insight into a person's own sense of security, their inclination to protect themselves, their property, and their loved ones – not minor considerations in this case.

So, we are having this little series of intimate chats with jurors who are being called up from the gallery before they are seated in the jury box, and I'm standing next to the Judge while looking down at my notes, and I hear Judge Fahey quietly mutter "Oh, oh." I look up and there's this 250 lb. guy dressed in a flannel shirt and red suspenders bounding up towards us and from his very flushed and sweaty look it's pretty clear that whatever he has to say he really can't hold his pee about it and we're about to hear something that's weighing heavily on his mind. And it's also pretty clear that he's not about to tell us that there's a half-price sale going on at the produce department at Wegman's.

Again, you need to remember that by this time in the festivities, the jurors have picked up smatterings, hints, and traces of what the Big Picture is here: a guy shoots another guy who's attacking him and his wife on the doorstep of their home. And the gun in question started out in the hands of the guy doing the attacking. So this florid faced giant comes up to us and just as the Judge is saying hello, the guy says, "Look, I been listenin' to this story all morning and you gotta know if some guy rushes me and my family with a gun, one of us ain't walking away. I don't know why this guy is even on trial, but I'm figurin' you oughtta know where I'm comin' from on this."

Even before the words "I'll take him" form on my lips, the Judge Fahey says, "Well thank you for sharing your thoughts with us sir. You're excused."

Notwithstanding the expected preconceived notions, slowly, we built a group of citizens who at least passed the "fair and impartial test." For all judges, that's the sole litmus test of getting seated on a jury. A guy could be sitting there in full Ku Klux Klan regalia and a Trump button on his robes and if he tells the judge, yes, he can be "fair and impartial" he gets seated. The parties still get to question the jurors and winnow out the oddballs or misfits and you still get "peremptory challenges" (in a murder case it's a fairly generous 20) which means you don't have to give a reason to exclude them. In the Peterson case we were getting a fairly standard cross section: a nurse, two teachers, a truck driver, an insurance salesman.

We were about halfway through (8 jurors seated) when I got a first act preview of Christine's version of her prosecutorial style. Given her performance during pretrial discovery, this should not have taken me aback or even surprised me, but still it was an unpleasant foretaste of things to come.

Both sides were reviewing their notes on the jurors who had just been questioned and I had pretty quickly decided I liked the fat guy wearing a tie and the retired teacher who was the grandmother of six. I still had plenty of peremptories left and the rest of these citizens were on my Do Not Fly list and if Christine didn't knock them off I would. So I'm ready to approach the bench and tell the Judge who I'm challenging. I look over at Christine and her co-counsel, the quietly efficient Melinda McGunnigle, and see that they are still deep in discussion of who's in, who's out.

Having a few minutes of downtime, I turn to Jeffrey and show him on my laptop computer what I think is the newest and coolest thing since the invention of the Slinky: Google Street View (remember, this is 2011). The internet had not yet caught up with courtroom technology so I had to bring my own Mi-Fi device and when I connected it to my laptop I was able to generate a 360° view of the corner of East Genesee and Ellis, up the street, down the street, wherever I wanted a witness to describe and where I wanted the jury to be looking. It was, in short, a cool tool. Jeffrey agreed.

Our quiet discussion of Google displays is interrupted by Christine standing up and announcing, "Judge, can we approach the bench?" I'm thinking, great, they are ready with their juror challenges. We approach the bench. I'm looking down at my notes, hoping that the prosecution is not going to knock off fat guy wearing tie and grandma of six, when Christine says, "Judge, I think Mr. Menkin is using the internet to look up juror backgrounds."

This statement had multiple levels of stunning. In the first place, unless I'm slipping fifties to the jurors, whatever else I'm doing on my side of the courtroom was entirely none of her business. In the second place, even if I was doing what she was complaining about, just one floor above us, the District Attorney's Office had a powerful computer network system sufficient to call up dates of birth, criminal records, DNA profiles, and favored shopping venues of every single person on the Commissioner of Jurors jury list if they wanted to. Beyond all of that, the complaint was downright juvenile.

Judge Fahey listened and didn't change his affect or expression. He just looked at me. I looked at him back. Knowing we each shared the same thought, he says "Hey Eddie, are you looking the jurors up on your computer?" I respond with an even "No" and Fahey says to Christine, "There you go." And there she went. But we were just getting started.

By the end of the day, we had a jury. And if they were expecting a great show, they got one.

Testimony: Who Can Tell the Better Story?

We had twelve jurors and a couple of alternates seated. The murder trial of The People of the State of New York v. Jeffrey Peterson was underway and anybody paying attention for more than fifteen minutes realized that this was to be a contest over who told the better story. The D.A., of course, had witnesses to tell their own versions of reality in the order the prosecution wants; but each side gets to question them and sometimes the defense's cross examination can turn what first sounds like The Exorcist into The Tale of Hansel & Gretel.

The jury we had picked sat expectantly, quietly, and attentive, perhaps somewhat unnerved by the two separate clans of families gathered on each side of the gallery, each to bear witness to the telling of the story that ended in disaster or death of their loved one. The Peterson family was, perhaps understandably, the larger of the two (Jeffrey, after all, had fathered eight children with a variety of women) and seemed to be better dressed and quieter than Shaheen Bean's clan, a group that had street written all over them. Each clan was led by a dominant mother, each the kind of woman whose affect and presence alone signaled a don't mess with me aura. Each had plenty to be unhappy about.

Besides the families, the trial attracted a large press contingent, an even larger clutch of defense lawyers and assistant D.A.s, and, curiously, to me, a surprising number of off duty detectives. I had first thought that the cops were there mainly to see to it that Jeffrey got his ticket permanently punched but, as it later turned out, I was very wrong on that score. They were hardly rooting for the defense, but there was another agenda at play there and it took a while for me to learn what that was.

We began the afternoon with opening statements. As I've said many times, you've got to tell the jury a story and your opening is the story. Beyond that, it is also the struggle between two lawyers over who is going to be the storyteller. It's all about shaping the narrative and since the prosecution always go first, if you are a defense attorney you need to seize the initiative from the get-go so that the jury is following you, not the D.A.

Every criminal trial has three stories, each running silently parallel alongside the others. The first isn't a story at all. It is the underlying event, the "reality." What actually happened. It's over, done, and in the past. The second story is called "Truth 1," the version of the event which the prosecutor wants to call a crime. The third story is how the defendant sees it. This is "Truth 2." Each side gets to tell its own story or at least say what is wrong about the other side's story.

It's a common wisdom, one overworked to the edge of triteness, that "a trial is the search for the truth." Judges say it, lawyers say it, professors profess it. But it really isn't. What it is is a contest between Truth 1 and Truth 2, whose story does the jury want to believe more?

So, we begin by telling our separate stories.

Christine's opening was pretty much the standard "table of contents of a book" preview of what was to come, and she did a pretty good job of laying out the prosecution's case and theory that this was about an "execution style murder." She told the jury that she had a witness to the execution, Debbie Kinsey, and they would hear from her. And she whetted the jury's appetite for the forensic proof to come, as if it was going to be this week's installment of "CSI Syracuse," describing the ballistic and blood spatter evidence they would hear, evidence which would leave no doubt that Jeffrey Peterson executed Shaheen Bean.

She did a competent and workmanlike job in laying out her case. Except for the part where she described Shaheen Bean as "a victim" and what happened on the Peterson's doorstep as an "encounter." I thought, presciently, that those references were a bit much and would eventually come back to bite her in the ass. Which they did.

My opening went full Power Point. The title card was marquee'd "A Case of Self-Defense" in large bold red letters and I took the jury, slide by slide, through the timeline of the 87 seconds and the 911 calls, referencing the events as they evolved and displaying police photographs of the scene, the keys in the open front door, the gun, Jeff Peterson's injuries and his clothing, his wife crying, and then concluding with a statement Jeffrey had made to the Grand Jury. ("I don't know if he came to kill, I don't know if he came to rob. All I knew was that he came with a gun and I just tried to do the best I could do to protect my wife and my family.") I wouldn't say that it was the greatest opening statement of my career, but it was organized, to the point, and got the job done. I mocked Christine's totally disingenuous description of Bean's attack on the Petersons as an "encounter" and suggested that an armed robber who got what he deserved shouldn't be anyone's idea of a "victim." It got the jury's attention and, more importantly, had them at least thinking about the possibility that this wasn't an execution but rather the story of a guy fighting for his life. Truth2.

Another thing you ought to know about how a trial unfolds is the profoundly underappreciated reality that no matter how the crime happened the jury is learning about it in the courtroom and over real time. That's why the order of witnesses is important.

In a murder case, a fairly standardized gambit is for the prosecution to open with the grieving survivor of the decedent, frequently a family member, to establish the identity of the person killed. But that's the collateral purpose. The real reason is to remind the jury of the life lost and the devastation visited on his or her loved ones. It's an effort to have the jury join in the mourning from the beginning of the story. When it's done right, it can have a powerful impact.

Christine wisely chose not to start this way. Notwithstanding her characterizing Bean as a "victim" in her opening, calling a family member to eulogize an armed robber wearing a doo rag and a mask and killed with his own gun was not the right psychological or emotional introduction to this story.

Instead, she wisely opted to go with the Uniform Opening. This is when the prosecution story opens with a witness in uniform, typically a cop. For one thing, a witness in uniform gets the jury's attention right away, especially if they have a badge and are carrying a gun. A witness in uniform invariably conveys the seriousness of the story they're about to hear. It could be a cop, an EMT, a military police officer, a jail guard. (I don't know how a mailman would play out as a first witness.) The point is to convey to the jury that whatever happened, it was something serious.

The D.A.'s first three witnesses were logical choices: the two cops first on the scene and the EMT who was a first responder from the Syracuse Fire Department. I liked this lineup. A lot. Without intending to, Christine allowed me to develop a common theme to their testimony: the scene at that dark early morning corner was one of apprehension, uncertainty, and danger, precisely the perceptions I wanted the jury to understand that Jeff Peterson was experiencing.

We first heard from Sgt. Todd Cramer who tells the jury that he is a road patrol supervisor and "a major crime scene coordinator." He received a call to respond to a "shooting with injury" at 04:43 hours (he doesn't know it, but bullets are still flying according to the 911 calls) and he arrives at 04:46, parking his cruiser a half a block up the street. He takes out his shotgun and approaches slowly and on foot. Because he's responding to the report of a shooting and it's dark and he doesn't know who's out there.

On cross examination, I made sure to connect what Cramer was thinking with what Jeff Peterson had to have been thinking. Peterson also doesn't 't know who else is out there. I also get Cramer to tell the jury that when he first encounters Peterson, who has his hands up (as does his wife), he said "They attacked me." This is pretty much the first the jury has heard on the subject of Bean having accomplices.

Cramer is followed by Officer Chris LaMontagne who

sees Bean lying on the ground and he has "no idea what's going on with him." I make it a point to get LaMontagne to tell the jury that even though it "appears" that "there wasn't much going on" with Bean, he still turned him over to check if he had a weapon. (If LaMontagne wondered, why wouldn't Peterson have the same apprehension?) Next is the EMT from the Syracuse Fire Department, John Abert, and he, unsurprisingly, assesses Bean as deceased; but also lets the jury know that even though Bean is quite dead there's still a degree of urgency to clear the scene since it's a shooting and "we don't quite know what's going on there." (Once again, a helpful comment for us.)

Mrs. Kinsey

It was now the time to explain "what was going on there." If Christine had a jackpot witness, it was Debbie Kinsey. Notwithstanding my belief that it was predominantly Fitz's zealotry that energized this prosecution of Jeff Peterson, in fairness it has to be said that he at least had something else to support his case: a witness. Mrs. Kinsey.

Bear in mind that our version of the event, our Truth2, was that Bean attacked Jeffrey and his wife in the 4:30 a.m. darkness and that in the struggle for Bean's gun while the two of them grappled on the ground, with the home security alarm wailing and Jeff's wife screaming a chorus of terror up on the porch, Bean took a round in the hip and then one in the head. Simple self-defense.

But while that was going on, across the street at 4:30 in the morning, was Mrs. Kinsey. She was getting her young grandson into her car, preparing for the long drive to New York City to see *The Lion King* on Broadway later that afternoon. She heard the commotion across the dark street, heard a gunshot, then another, and, incredibly, moved towards the figures battling on the ground on the lawn of the house on the corner. Bravely, she called 911 and, in a one in a million happenstance, she was actually narrating what she thought she was seeing to the 911 operator by the time the last shot goes off (which you could clearly hear on the call).

She's on the phone, she's still 75 feet away in the middle of the darkened street (the corner streetlight was out), and she's soulfully calling out, "We comin' for you baby! Help's comin'." The tragic fact that Mrs. Kinsey had previously lost a son to a street shooting had to have colored her perception of what she was seeing. There's no doubt that she was picking up the whole drama up midcourse (our chart of the times of the 911 calls made that clear), and she really had no idea if it was Bean or Jeffrey who was the "baby" who needed help. All of this was, of course, recorded and available on CD which Christine helpfully played for the jury.

According to Mrs. Kinsey, there's the struggle (pretty much as we envisioned it), a gunshot while Jeff and Bean were on the ground (in Fitz's version of reality, this was the shot to Bean's hip which disabled him), and then, according to her, Jeff gets up and offs Bean by shooting him in the head while standing over him.

Even if Mrs. Kinsey is completely accurate, my reaction is: – yeah? and so? And I was willing to bet that 12 people even randomly picked off the street would see it that way. The D.A., on the other hand, saw the event as an act of legitimate but colorable self-defense which rapidly turns into an execution.

I wasn't looking forward to cross-examining Mrs. Kinsey.

She was, after all, acting as a good citizen in making the call in the first place. And having herself lost a son to gunfire made her an especially sympathetic figure. And could there be anything more endearing than taking your grandson to see *The Lion King*? I decided not to attack her in any way – after all, where was I going with that approach? – but instead decided to ask about the limits of what it was that she could really see and understand.

It wasn't lost on me, and I made sure that it wasn't lost on the jury, that when her husband heard the commotion and the first gunshot, she was inside the house. And when the police interviewed her husband, Mr. Kinsey, who had first called her attention to the turmoil across the street, the investigator reported that, "I looked in the direction of the scene from where [Mr.] Kinsey described as the area where he was standing. It was approximately sixty yards from the scene to Kinsey's driveway. The area in which this incident took place, was down a small knoll in Peterson's yard, which made it difficult to clearly see what was happening from where Kinsey was standing at the time of this incident."

Given the distances and timing, it was pretty obvious that whatever Mrs. Kinsey saw was entirely shaped by the fact that she was inside her own home when it started, that she was at least 60 yards from the scene when she first came out onto her driveway, that she couldn't see - much less understand - what was happening on the dark lawn across the street, and that whatever it was she was coming on to, it was in the middle of the episode.

It also didn't help reinforce her reliability as a witness that on the phone call she got some of the details of the things right in front of her wrong: the color and pattern of Jeffrey's shirt; the color of the Peterson house; the names of the streets intersecting at the corner; the color of the gun; not being sure if it was a gun at all.

The point was not to show that she was lying or wrong – she certainly wasn't lying – but rather to show that the drama unfolding in front of her in the darkness was of such a heightened intensity that she was losing the ability to think objectively and rationally. Sort of like my client who was in a frenzied struggle for his life while facing the business end of a gun and grappling with the gunman on the ground. The jury got the picture.

There was another reason I needed to keep my distance from Debbie Kinsey: despite the fact that Jeffrey and his wife lived literally across the street, she didn't know him. And, much more to the point, she couldn't and didn't identify him as the guy with "the silver gun" (it was mostly black and on the 911 call it is pretty clear that she's not even sure it's a gun in the first place). She had the shooter wearing a short-sleeved cream-colored shirt. The jury knew that Jeff was wearing a purple and white checked long sleeved dress shirt. (And that became important much later in the trial when we got to the "blood spatter evidence.")

Despite what you see on TV, sometimes on cross examination less is better. My questions for Debbie Kinsey did not go on for much more than ten minutes and what she didn't say was more important for me than what she did.

Reasonable doubt is a doubt founded on a reason. Debbie Kinsey gave the jury that reason. She wasn't the closer that the DA had hoped for.

Detective Hack

After Debbie Kinsey testified, it was time for another Badge, an important one. Christine next called Detective George Hack, the officer who interviewed Jeff Peterson just a few hours after the shooting. Hack was an affable type, with a personality much like your kid's high school soccer coach (except your kid's soccer coach probably wouldn't send his team out to cripple the opponent's midfielder if he thought that kid was committing too many fouls). He was an articulate guy who was pretty good at talking to people. Not all cops have this skill but those who do, like Hack, are very good at it.

Having reported to work at 8:00 a.m. the morning of the shooting, he was fresh and well rested and it didn't seem to bother him at all that he would be interviewing a guy who had already gone without sleep for at least 24 hours and just been involved in a fist fight and a fatal shooting. He met with Jeff in a mirrored interview room. Sal was there (having been called by Jeff's mother), but on the other side of the mirror were a clutch of police officers and an assistant D.A. who were strategizing, debating, and just plain figuring out how best to get the "truth" from this guy who they all regarded as a major O.G. but who could also conceivably have actually acted in self-defense. They would from time to time brief Detective Hack on the fly as more information was flowing in from the scene and from the investigation, which was still at its earliest stages. In another room down the hall, Jeff Peterson's wife was also being interviewed.

After about three hours of earnest and generally "friendly" discussion, Jeff Peterson confirmed everything he had told

Hack in a single-spaced two-page typed statement. Hack read it to the jury:

I, Jeffrey D. Peterson, being duly sworn, state I am thirty-nine years of age, and my address is 2501 East Genesee Street, Syracuse, New York. My occupation is N/A and I have completed twelve years of school. ["Q. What is N/A? A. Nonapplicable, meaning he doesn't work."] I can be reached at the following phone numbers, 315-378-**** and there is no work number. It is 9:45 a.m. on June 26th, 2010, and I am giving this statement to Syracuse Police Detective George Hack while at the Syracuse Police Department Criminal Investigations Division. I have been advised of my constitutional rights, while my Attorney, Sal Piemonte, is present. At the advice of Mr. Piemonte, I am giving this statement on my own free will and without any promises. This statement is true.

At about 4:40 a.m. on June 26th, 2010, I was unlocking my door at my house, located at 2501 East Genesee Street in the city of Syracuse as my wife was behind me. I was standing on the porch on the side of the house with the key in the door as she was on the step. All of a sudden my wife was screaming. I looked over my right shoulder and I saw a guy standing behind her with a gun in his hand, and I think he was wearing a mask over his face. I flung open the door to the house, hoping that the alarm would go off. I turned and dove off the porch towards him, I started fighting with him, tussling for the gun. He was yelling, homey, homey, like he was yelling for help. We went to the ground and I was on the side of him trying to hold on to his arms. He was trying to point the gun at me, then all of a sudden I heard gunshots. At some point while we were fighting he bit my right arm and I bit one of his hands as hard as I could. I think it was the hand that had the gun in it. When I heard the gunshots, I did not hear my wife screaming anymore and I thought that he shot her. We kept fighting and I kept hearing gunshots. I don't know how many gunshots I heard. We kept fighting until he stopped moving. When he stopped moving, I was able to get the gun out of the guy's hand. I got off of him and heaved the gun into the street. I yelled to my wife to call 9-1-1, then I went up on the porch and into the house. When I went into the house, I took my purple and white checkered button-down shirt off and tossed it on the couch. I wanted to get the police there as fast as I could, so I kept yelling for her to call 9-1-1. I kept looking out the window to see if they were there yet. One of the times I looked out I saw an older dark colored SUV, maybe a Ford Explorer, drive up Ellis Street real slow. I saw two black guys in it. They were looking towards my house like they were checking to see what happened. My wife yelled to those guys to call 9-1-1, but I told her not say that to them because I thought they were with the guy I just fought with. I don't know which way they turned on Genesee street. Shortly after I went back outside. I was standing near the porch when I saw the first police officer walk up towards us with a shotgun. He put me in the back of a police van, then drove me down the street. We sat there for a while, then they brought me to the police station. When we got to the police station I told the police that I wanted to speak to my attorney, Mr. Piemonte. When I got to the police station, I pointed out to the police I had a bite mark on my right tricep where the guy bit me. I also had bump on the left side of my head and cuts on both of my hands. My pants were also muddy on both legs from the knees down. I did not have any of those injuries and my pants were clean before I was attacked. The police took picture of my injuries and dirty pants. I do not know the guy who attacked me. When the police told me that his name was Shaheen Bean and that he died from a gunshot wound, I did not know him and I have never heard of him. It seemed like this thing happened in just seconds, I am telling Detective Hack what happened to the best of my recollection. I know that since Shaheen died the police have to do a thorough investigation. I give them consent to search my house for anything that they might think is related to the investigation and have signed a consent. I have read the statement and it is the truth.

Now, having Hack read this statement from the stand was the first opportunity the jury had to actually hear in Jeff Peterson's words, not his lawyer's or anyone else's, his version of the night's events. I knew, as Christine surely knew, that there wasn't a chance that Jeffrey was going to testify in his own defense, so it wasn't necessarily to our disadvantage to having Detective Hack give his reading of Jeff's story.

Christine's purpose, of course, was to try and convince the jury that this version was false and that Peterson had lied to the police from the get-go. (The legal term is "false exculpatory statement.") Technically, I could have objected to Hack reading the statement on the grounds that it was hearsay because it didn't come within the hearsay exception of being an "admission or confession." Under the law, an "admission" is a party's statement which is inconsistent with his position at trial. This wasn't any such thing. It certainly didn't rise to the level of a "confession" since Jeff Peterson was not acknowledging that he had committed a crime.

There were a number of positives we derived from the jury hearing this statement. In the first place - and this was psychologically important - it showed that Jeff Peterson was cooperative with the police. Even though he was injured, sleep deprived, and had just engaged in a furious struggle leaving a man dead, he talked freely with Hack for three or four hours. Having his lawyer present didn't count as an act of evasion. He consented to having the police search his home. He consented to the police photographing him and taking some of his clothing. They could have gotten search warrants to do all that, but he agreed without any procedural complication. Would a man who was hiding something agree to all that?

His statement also made it clear that Peterson did not think that his assailant was acting alone. Our Plan B was no longer Plan B, it was up front and center in our defense: Bean called out "homey, homey!" (calling for aid?) and the two guys slowly rolling up Ellis in a black SUV right after the shooting and not responding with help or calling 911 strongly suggested that Bean had accomplices.

Jeff's statement that he was the one on the upper level of the porch when Bean attacked was demonstrably incorrect but that really didn't harm us very much. Detective Hack showed him that the set of keys found in the door at the scene belonged to Peterson's wife and that caused Jeff to amend the statement and give a short second one. No harm, no foul, and an understandable omission under the circumstances.

I liked Hack (he was a personable guy) but only up to a point. There he was in a closed room interviewing someone he surely thought of as a street gangster who had just committed a homicide. He actually yearned to lock Jeffrey up then and there but couldn't do so because the higher ups in the Department were not yet sure where either they or the D.A. wanted to take this. As far as Hack was concerned, Jeff Peterson was no victim. But there he was in a closed room with Jeff Peterson and his lawyer taking Jeffrey's "victim statement." And Hack was getting directives from behind the mirror every 15 minutes or so: ask Peterson this, that, photograph his body, take his shirt, his pants.

Whether it was Hack's fault (I think not) or somebody else's oversight, no one thought to take Jeff Peterson's white sneakers. They were very new and very white and if, as the police theorized (and Mrs. Kinsey seemed to confirm), Jeff Peterson stood right over Shaheen Bean and put a bullet in the guy's head there almost certainly would have been blood spatter "castoff" showing on these kicks. The police already had the gun and it didn't take an electron microscope to see that there were specks of blood on the muzzle. But the photos the police took of Jeffrey's clothing didn't do much good in proving Debbie Kinsey's story of Peterson standing over Bean when he shot him in the head. Whatever glimpses of his footwear were captured in the photos did not show any blood.

Whether the failure to take Peterson's sneakers was Hack's fault or not, I still wanted to portray the detective as a guy with an agenda, one shared by the police, which was poorly executed and wrongheaded and one which led to an unfair prosecution. Hack himself provided me with a small opportunity.

He had questioned Peterson early on Saturday morning June 26 but didn't arrest him even though he thought the guy was a criminal. Some weeks later, Jeffrey Peterson voluntarily appeared before the Grand Jury to tell his side of the story. That was on Friday morning, July 23 and, not knowing that right after his testimony the Grand Jury voted to indict him for Bean's murder, he and his wife then went to the movies that afternoon. When the Petersons came out of the movie, Hack was waiting for Jeffrey in the lobby with a set of handcuffs, telling him "Things have changed. I got you now." The remark, which he admitted making, made him look petty and vindictive to the jury and you could tell that they didn't like it

On that note, Day Two of the Peterson trial adjourned for the morrow.

Sidebar Drama

The first two days of the trial may have appeared to some of the spectators to be high drama. And it was. And it was certainly stressful and a lot of work. But mostly hidden from the jury, and barely discernible to the gallery, was a sidebar minidrama which was starting to have consequences: the rising tide of tension between Christine and me. The nonsense over juror lookups was only a prologue.

It's never a good idea to let your irritation and anger at your adversary's behavior get out front and into public display. For one thing, of course, the trial isn't about you or them it's about your client. And for another, although it might be an amusing side show for the spectators, if the side show becomes the main show the verdict becomes a referendum on who got the best of whom. Still, she was pissing me off. Big time.

Christine had been difficult enough to deal with through discovery, but it wasn't until the trial got underway that I came to a full appreciation of her unique litigation style. It really started with her witness list. Fifty-two witnesses. Yes, it was a murder case, and, yes, it had some unusual aspects to it. But the underlying event took 87 seconds and there were only three people involved at the scene (four if you counted Mr. Bean but he was permanently unavailable to testify). She's gonna call 52 witnesses? This wasn't the Warren Commission investigation into the JFK assassination. Fifty-two witnesses meant, for us, preparation of fifty-two cross examinations. On one day's notice.

Okay, I'm thinking, we know as much as she does about what happened here, maybe more. Maybe she's being obsessively prepared. We'll have to deal with it. So, it's the end of the second day, we are done with Detective Hack, the sixth witness in a purported list of fifty-two. We are gathering our files and exhibits and while Sal is chatting up Tim McCarthy, the affable D.A.'s investigator, showing him this really cool composite graphic exhibit that I had put together, I turn to Christine and ask her what her witness order for tomorrow is like. This is a basic and routine courtesy engaged in by all trial lawyers, second only to standing up when the Judge enters the courtroom. She says, "I don't have to tell you that." Which, of course, was true, as true perhaps as the possibility that a defense lawyer could stand up in front of the jury and ask them to convict his client. It's unheard of and just not done. For one thing, it's simple courtesy; for another, it saves everybody's time because it allows your adversary to more efficiently prepare (something which apparently didn't sit well with Christine). There's really no good reason to withhold the witnesses' order unless there's a compelling need to adhere to gamesmanship.

The stress of the day, and the burden of the case, get to me. I erupt in a cascade of anger, just short of profanity (something unusual for me; yelling is not my thing, even with my children, but when I'm upset, profanity is, I regret to say, my lingua franca).

There's a reporter in the room, scribbling furiously, and I look over to Sal who's still chirping away with McCarthy, giving him an unwarranted preview of a really cool exhibit we've put together. I channel my fury at Sal, barking at him to shut the fuck up, pick up the rest of our stuff, and join me in leaving now. Steam is blowing from my every orifice. I myself am perilously close to violating the Trial Lawyer's Eleventh Commandment promulgated by my friend Robbie Wells, trial lawyer extraordinaire: "Thou Shalt Not Be a Dick." This was not my finest show of professionalism and it certainly didn't make me feel any better. In fact it made me feel worse that Christine had finally found a button she could push. Hate it when an opponent has your number.

A Curveball from the Jury Box

Every trial that goes on for more than a few days has a curveball moment, something unexpected that upends things for a while. Three jurors getting sick at the same time, an important witness does a 180 on the party who called him, two lawyers getting into a fist fight (actually happened), could be anything. A trial is, after all, a dynamic in human behavior and there's really nothing predictable about these events as they are unfolding.

In the Peterson trial, it didn't take long for our first curveball moment. We were in Day 4, and apart from my squabbling with Christine things were going pretty smoothly as far as I was concerned. We were getting ready for the afternoon session when the Judge's clerk comes out to say we are wanted in chambers. Not a welcome sign.

We all trundle off to Judge Fahey's chambers and encounter the ever-smiling Joe in his robes and leaning back in his chair. "You're not gonna believe this." His remark, somewhat to both my mild embarrassment and amusement, is directed to me, a further sign (one of several so far) that Christine is mainly a bystander to an ongoing conversation Joe and I had been having discussing the unfolding case of the People of the State of New York v. Jeffrey Peterson. Alternate Juror #2 had decided it was important to pay the Judge a visit and to disclose an overheard remark one of the seated jurors had made. Curveball.

Alternate Juror #2 had already garnered my attention. She was an intense academic who was clearly thrilled to be on this jury, was following everything with a hawk-like vigilance, and had been engaged in constant notetaking as if she was Della Street furiously taking dictation from Perry Mason. I don't mind if jurors take notes; some judges actually encourage it. The downside is that once deliberations begin, the most prolific note taker can start to drive the conversation in the jury room and instead of depending on the evidence and testimony which can be read back to them by the court reporter, the jurors defer to this "record."

I noticed AJ#2's furious note-taking right away and had the embarrassingly self-serving thought that this woman was going to beat me to the punch and write a book about this trial before I had the chance to do it myself. (It's now some eight years later and I haven't seen her work listed on the NYT Best Seller List.) I was curious, along with everybody else, about what she wanted to talk to the Judge about.

AJ#2 was ushered into the Judge's chambers. She was small, expectedly nervous, and right away apologized for disturbing us. Joe set her at ease and asked her to tell the lawyers what she had overheard. "Well, it was after the break yesterday, and we were walking down the hallway, and Juror #3 said something like- and please forgive me for repeating it- 'What do I give a shit about one black guy shooting another black guy?' I thought you ought to know."

Joe asked us if we had any questions. I asked her if Juror #3 had actually said it to anyone specific or if anyone had responded. No, she said, it was just a remark made during the short parade back to the jury room. Nobody responded or followed up as far as she knew.

There being an awkward few moments of silence and no one else having any questions, Joe excused her and asked her to keep all of this to herself. (She had discretely been called into the Judge's chambers and the other jurors most probably thought she was on a bathroom break.)

I'm momentarily entertaining the stray thought that maybe the guy didn't say anything remotely like this at all and that this is AJ#2's maneuver to get on the deliberating jury and not just remain on deck. I'm also thinking that maybe a different version of the red suspender guy had worked his way onto this jury.

The Judge sends for Juror #3, a trim, middle aged guy, a trucker who lived in the blue-collar suburbs just south of the City. He comes in smiling, acting as if we're going to discuss last night's Yankees game. Joe tells him that the remark he made yesterday in the hallway about one black guy shooting another was overheard and reported to him. In an even tone, Joe asks him if that's what he actually said. The guy doesn't miss a beat or change his affect. He smiles and says "Yeah, I said that. I was just joking around. I probably shouldn't have."

Joe asks him if he has prejudged this case. He says no. Joe asks him if he's discussed the case with anyone else. Guy says no. Joe asks him if he can be fair and impartial and keep an open mind. The guy says yes.

Joe asks us if we have any questions for #3. Astoundingly, Christine says no. It apparently doesn't occur to her to ask if the guy would view this case differently if the fight and shootout was between two white guys. Or maybe a black guy and a white guy. Or maybe ask him if he thinks black people in this situation should be judged by some different standard. Okay, I'm thinking, the situation is uncomfortable and sensitive enough that she's not going to embarrass anyone by asking this affable racist if he is a racist; she'll just wait until he's out of the room and ask the Judge to get rid of him. I really don't know what she's thinking.

I don't have any questions for the guy since a) it's pretty clear he doesn't care that Shaheen Bean is dead (a disreputable plus for our side), and b) it doesn't matter what else I ask because Christine is clearly going to get rid of him.

So #3 is sent back to the jury room. We wait until the

door is closed and he is out of earshot. Joe turns to Christine and asks her if she wants to challenge and dismiss #3. She says "no." I look over to Joe, Joe looks over to me. We are both having out of body experiences.

He asks me if I want to dismiss him. The tiny evil elf named Mr. Cynicism behind my ear is whispering "This is not so bad." Thinking, in part, I'm way better off having #3 sitting there than possibly the obsessive note-taking snitch AJ#2 in his place and that the guy really couldn't be all that bad for my side if he's generally OK with Bean being dead, I say "no."

The Judge could, if he wanted to, dismiss the guy on his own initiative, but it's a truism of litigation that the parties are entitled to chart their own trial and have the juries they want to decide their client's fate. So Joe leaves things as they are and sends us back to the courtroom where we can await the next curveball moment.

Later that afternoon, I notice that AJ#2 has started work on a new notebook.

"As Seen on T.V."

Americans are obsessed with television. More people know the names of the characters on "The Big Bang Theory" than the names of their own representatives in Congress. Donald Trump has been known to select Cabinet officials and advisors predominantly because he likes the way they come across on T.V. Jurors aren't any different. Their impressions of the law and courtroom procedure come almost exclusively from what they've seen on television, and their expectations of what role science has in the law has been overwhelmingly influenced by the wildly popular "CSI" series broadcast on CBS.

"The CSI Effect" is a well-established and well documented phenomenon in scores of serious legal studies. Jurors are psychologically primed and inclined to expect to be convinced by forensic evidence. Forensic experts are frequently determinative to the outcome of criminal cases, most particularly when it comes to DNA evidence. (Not always, of course; ask O.J. Simpson.)

But if the prosecution starts to dwell too long on the minutia of forensic evidence, as started to happen in the Peterson case, then the jury loses the thread of The Story. The prosecution's Truth 1 starts to get less truthier.

Refried Confusion Isn't Making Itself Clear

Maybe it was a case of the D.A. and the police wanting to satisfy the jury's CSI Effect curiosity or to show them how much work they had put into the case, but for several mid-trial days, the Peterson case turned into Forensics on Parade. Except the parade started marching around in a widening circle, crashing into itself, and didn't appear to have a destination. The prosecution's expert witness testimony was certainly educational, but it wasn't serving much purpose. Muhammad Ali famously showcased the Ali Shuffle, a series of moves where he danced around the ring; but, as Ali well knew, if he never delivered a body blow to his opponent, all it did was tire him out.

The jury was inundated with interesting testimony from interesting people. What it proved, however, was open to question. Some of the forensic testimony raised more questions than we started with, never a good turn of events for a prosecutor.

Take, for instance, Detective Terry McGinn, an affable and knowledgeable Irishman who was the Syracuse Police Lab's Renaissance Man when it came to analyzing evidence. You want fingerprint analysis? DNA interpretation? blood stain pattern analysis? trace evidence? gunshot residue explanations? firearms analysis? McGinn was your guy. He was a complete season of CSI in one witness.

McGinn walked the jury through the multitude of photos and a DVD of the scene (by the time his testimony was done there were well over 75 prosecution exhibits admitted into evidence). McGinn gave the jury a tour of the yellow plastic evidence markers dotting the Petersons' side lawn and located the spots where bullet casings were found. Just when we were on the verge of the jury finding out at least where the gun was when the shots rang out, McGinn almost gratuitously added that the location of the shells does not necessarily indicate the position of the gun when it was fired. I guess that is useful information if you are writing a Wiki entry on gunfire, but why did we need the tour of yellow evidence markers?

He expertly displayed the gun and pronounced it an operable weapon (a real shocker; who would have guessed?). This 9mm Ruger semiautomatic pistol was a particularly nasty little piece of equipment. It had a magazine with a 12-round capacity and there were 5 live rounds (hollow points) still in it when it was recovered with the safety off. A shell was jammed in the ejection port and McGinn explained "stovepiping" to the jury. Could have been a faulty ejector (but the gun had fired at least 4 bullets); could have been a squib round or a slide malfunction; or there could have been something obstructing ejection. We were particularly happy to have that last piece of testimony as we had a somewhat interesting explanation of that when the Medical Examiner, Dr. Philip, took the stand.

McGinn pointed out that there was "back spatter" blood on the tip of the barrel and left side of the ejection port, and that there was hair on the tip. As evidence goes, I would say that was pretty convincing that somebody got shot in the head with this gun. And later testimony established that the hair and the blood belonged to Bean. (Another shock.) But the mystery in the case – if there really was a "mystery" – wasn't whether this 9mm was the "murder weapon"; Bean quite obviously was shot in the head with the gun. The real mystery was whether this was a murder at all.

A murder needs a murderer. And a murderer needs a murder weapon. Connecting Bean to the gun was simplistic child's play. His blood, hair, and DNA were on it. The prosecution didn't need its cast of forensic characters to connect the gun to their "victim"; what they needed was to tie Jeffrey Peterson to the gun. The closer Christine's witnesses got to the question of whether Jeffrey Peterson had actually wielded the gun at all (notwithstanding Debbie Kinsey's testimony) the more questions arose.

You may recall that in Jeff Peterson's detailed statement to Detective Hack he never once acknowledged firing the gun ("I started fighting with him, tussling for the gun. . . . He was trying to point the gun at me, then all a sudden I heard gunshots. . . . When he stopped moving, I was able to get the gun out of the guy's hand. I got off of him and heaved the gun into the street.").

So it had to be somewhat of a puzzlement for the jury to listen to the D.A. day after day argue that Peterson shot Bean but at the same time hear from the lab's forensic scientists,

Marie Guido and Tamara Danner, that there was no gunshot residue found on Jeffrey Peterson or his clothing; that there were three DNA contributors found on the frame of the gun; that there were no usable fingerprints found on the gun; that there was no blood on Jeff Peterson's pants and sneakers; and that the only trace of Bean's blood on Peterson's clothing was found on the right cuff of his long-sleeved shirt (which didn't do much to prove that Peterson had fired the gun, especially because after having him in their full view just feet away during the two week trial, it was obvious to the jury that Jeffrey Peterson was left-handed).

So after four full days of forensic testimony from seven different CSI witnesses on the subject of how science can solve crimes, the jury was left wondering who was the third DNA contributor to the gun? Why were there no fingerprints (always a jury favorite no matter the crime)? Where was there any forensic proof that Jeffrey Peterson actually fired the gun? And to compound the prosecution's growing dilemma, if you carefully listened to all this forensic proof, the defense's suggestion that Bean actually could have shot himself during the struggle no longer seemed so far-fetched.

It was pretty obvious that the prosecution's plan was to call these forensic witnesses to lay an evidentiary foundation so they could wind their case up with their two forensic Big Guns: the Medical Examiner who performed Bean's autopsy, and their blood spatter expert who would explain why specks of blood on Peterson's right cuff showed he fired the gun even though Peterson was left-handed.

At least that was the plan. And as Mike Tyson once famously said, "Everybody has a plan until they get punched in the mouth."

The Dentist on the Courtroom Floor

If you've read this far into this saga, you'll realize that modesty is not my long suit. I know this. I know that there are some people who follow my so-called career and feel some degree of pleasure or amusement (I'd like to think awe) at my occasional forays into performance art. There's little doubt that a lot of trial work, at least the way I practice it, is a version of theater. Although I don't carry around my personal makeup kit, I know that I'm ever prepared to rise to the role as circumstances present themselves.

One time Dustin Hoffman was on the set of "Marathon Man" talking to the great Laurence Olivier and he asked Sir Larry what he thought about why actors act. Olivier burst dramatically into Hoffman's face and, with his eyes wide, blurted out "Look at me, Look at me, Look at me!" Same can be said about trial lawyers. Definitely me.

Many years ago, I was going to trial on a medical malpractice case and we had picked a jury. The facts were really bizarre, the doctor outrageously negligent, and my client's damages were very, very real. Unfortunately, we had drawn the laziest judge in five counties and the jury panel resembled the Cantina bar scene from Star Wars. (The case was in Utica. Enough said on that score.) The judge was leaning heavily on me to settle and go away so he could play some golf, and there was a very substantial amount of money on the table. My client, a sweet demure woman, talked it over with her husband and decided to settle.

We went through the required motions and rituals in front of the judge who could now pack up his golf clubs. I packed up my trial briefcase, files, and exhibits getting ready to drive back to Syracuse a much richer lawyer than I had started out that morning.

My client comes up to me and says, "You're disappointed, aren't you?" I said no, you did the right thing by settling.

She says, "You really wanted to try the case, didn't you?"

I paused for a second, and said to her, "Well, Barb, what I really wanted was a starring role in a longer movie."

Well, by Day # 8 the Jeffrey Peterson case was playing to packed houses and sock-o reviews and the starring role I'm always looking for was receiving IMAX treatment. It was, as I always envisioned it was going to be, just me in the center of the arena doing battle with the inept forces of prosecutorial darkness, kicking ass here and taking names there. There are precious few trial cases that come your way where everything breaks in your favor. This was one of them.

One of the more fortuitous breaks came in the person of Dr. Abraham Philip, the forensic pathologist who performed the autopsy of the unfortunate Mr. Bean. Dr. Philip was a temporary hire on a short-term contract with the Onondaga County Medical Examiner's Office. His previous employment with the Chief Medical Examiner of the State of Massachusetts ended rather poorly for him. Dr. Philip had somehow managed to turn a death certificate requested by a funeral director into a biohazard (by getting blood on it) and then aggravated his supervisor by suggesting that a female Assistant District Attorney who had been giving him a hard time had conspired to accuse him of farting on a homicide file Dr. Philip needed to review. After losing his lawsuit for discriminatory termination, he prudently decided to explore new opportunities in Onondaga County.

Despite the rather bizarre baggage Dr. Philip brought

along with him, he was a bright man with a low-key but pleasing affect on the stand, and he testified pretty straightforwardly that the gunshot of a hollow point bullet into the back of Mr. Bean's head had ended his life. Cause of death: homicide. Of course, all due respect to Dr. Philip, a kid in junior high school could have donned a white lab coat, taken the stand, and testified to the same opinion without much fear of contradiction.

Since it's pretty hard for a prosecutor to get a conviction in a murder case without proving that the victim is dead, calling the Medical Examiner who performed the autopsy on the recently departed is as basic as it gets. Frequently, it's a short Q and A without much challenge, drama, or complexity. Dead is dead. There are some cases where the cause of death is seriously called into question (I've had a few), but in the Jeffrey Peterson case a hollow point bullet to the head speaks for itself. The bigger question, and the reason I was looking forward to cross-examining Dr. Philip, had everything to do with how it got there.

Now, you need to remember that Bean was shot twice: he took one in the hip and one in the head. From, of course, his own gun. Fitz's theory was that the hip wound was sufficiently disabling that there was no need for Jeffrey to get up and off the guy with a *coup de grâce* to the head. As far as Fitz was concerned, Jeff's justified self-defense ended with the hip shot and what followed was a pretty straightforward execution murder. Christine's opening statement to the jury made it clear that was the story, and, of course, she had Mrs. Kinsey's version of the struggle to support that theory even though she was 75 feet away in the darkness.

But Fitz being Fitz and a devoted belt and suspenders kind

of guy, he wanted to hammer that theory down with six-inch nails and then pour a load of concrete over it. Much to Fitz's delight, Dr. Philip was happy to oblige with his own forensic toolkit, and early in the investigation he had solemnly opined before the Grand Jury that Bean's hip wound was sustained before the head shot:

Q. Are you able to give an opinion with a reasonable degree of medical certainty in which order the gunshots were sustained?

A. *It is my opinion that the gunshot wound to the thigh was sustained first.*

Now, I didn't go to medical school, but in my judgment Dr. Philips' testimony on this point was somewhat the equivalent of an allegedly well-credentialed expert witness telling the jury that after his years of study, experience, and peer reviewed journal research, he was absolutely certain that the chicken had indeed come before the egg. No question about it.

It had seemed to me that there was a serious question about it, and I had spent a considerable number of hours outlining a set of questions to show that Dr. Philip did not know what he was talking about. His theory had all the forensic scientific validity of predicting a coin flip. It's pretty easy, I'll admit, to tell if a wound is a postmortem injury (lack of bleeding is an obvious clue). But it is virtually impossible to tell which of two nearly simultaneous gunshot wounds came before the other. So, I put down the cross examination of Dr. Philip as one of my featured acts in the drama to come. I was really looking forward to it.

Didn't happen. And the reason it didn't happen was just one more confirmation that the spheres of good fortune and fate were smiling down on Jeff Peterson and his lawyer (that would be me).

About two weeks before the start of the trial, I got a call from Christine. Would I mind holding until Fitz gets on the line? My interest is piqued. The King of New York his own very self is about to grant me some few precious moments of time. And he wants to talk to me! Thrilling. Whatever this is about, I know it's going to be of more than passing interest. And it was.

It turns out that in preparing for trial they had given Dr. Philip a copy of his Grand Jury testimony, and he read for himself what he had previously offered as his expert opinion. I wasn't in the room when he read it, but I can predict with a high degree of confidence that his main response was "I really said that?" To his credit (and I'm envisioning Fitz's reaction being something which probably hovered between disappointment and rage), Dr. Philip decided that his theory wasn't actually ready for prime time and he couldn't bring himself to testify at trial which shot had preceded the other. Fitz and Christine felt obligated, undoubtedly by the finest traditions of ethical criminal prosecution standards, to disclose this to me. Ya think?

A couple of minutes of nearly comic posturing then ensued on the phone. They charitably and high mindedly offered to dismiss the indictment (sounds great doesn't it?) so they could re-present the case "more fairly" to a new Grand Jury (maybe not so good) and we can then see what they decide to do (not liking those odds). It would be my call. I pretended to think about it. Let's see: should I go to trial when a key witness for the prosecution has just done a 180 on them, taken a shit over their seminal theory, and would be limping around the courtroom as if he had just had an intimate encounter with Mike Tyson's right uppercut, or should I go tell Jeffrey that I decided to give Fitz another chance to patch up his broke-ass case so Jeff might still be convicted of murder? Nah. Thanks for the high-minded disclosure my friends, but I think we're good. Let's keep the trial date.

So now we're at trial, and the newly ethically endowed Dr. Philip is on the stand, and my outline pages of what would have been a brilliant cross-examination on which of the two shots came first are useless to me. I frequently tell young lawyers (when they ask about what it takes to go to trial) that once you are underway and in the courtroom you need to act like you're never gonna run out of aces. No matter what. Well, in this case, I still did have an ace to play: my neighbor and friend Cliff, an 80-year-old retired dentist.

Cliff was a widower with a quiet manner and a great sense of humor. He always seemed to be up for one kind of adventure or another and had literally traveled the world in his retirement (Galapagos, Vietnam, the Far West). And he was a faithful contributor to our morning coffee group at the local bagelry, a disparate group consisting of (depending on the day of the week) a real estate broker, a farmer, a funeral director, a sitting City Court Judge, a marina owner, an engineer who was a graduate of the Naval Academy, and a teacher. Suffice to say, if I was ever in need of the opinion of a mock jury made up of a reasonable cross section of the community, they were a reliable and readymade focus group. Besides that, they almost always enjoyed my trial stories which I was never reticent about sharing. They were eagerly following the Jeff Peterson case and ever ready to offer supportive tips, opinions, and views. A few of them actually came down during the day to watch the trial.

Ever one to maximize an audience, one day it dawned on me that my dentist pal Cliff was the same height as Jeff Peterson. And, as it happened, so was I. And, as circumstance would have it, the three of us were the same height as the late Shaheen Bean. The 5'9" club. So, with that in mind, I devised a small demonstration which I had rehearsed with Cliff and I asked the Judge if it would be all right if I cross-examined Dr. Philip by asking him to watch a re-enactment performed by me and Cliff. My intention was to then ask him if it was possible that the struggle on the ground between Peterson and Bean could have resulted in Bean shooting himself in the head.

Christine, of course, was having kittens at the prosecution table protesting how preposterous this all was, but Judge Fahey was amused by the whole thing (as I knew he would be) and gave me the OK.

So I rolled out a sheet of polyethylene and put it on the floor in front of the witness and the jury and I called Cliff up from the gallery. He laid down, supine, playing the part of the soon to be departed Mr. Bean, just as we had rehearsed. I gave him a make-believe gun that I had fashioned from some wood left over from my kid's pinewood derby project. The dimensions were to spec, the same length and shape as Bean's 9mm. When Cliff grasped the wooden gun in his left hand, I laid on top of him (in the role of Jeff P) and we were face to face and belly to belly. I pretended to restrain his left hand with my right hand, and when Cliff turned his face away to his right, I asked the quietly stunned Dr. Philip if it was true that in the configuration we were presenting wasn't it possible that the gun in Bean's hand could have gone off and that it was Bean who had actually inflicted the fatal shot into his own head.

Dr. Philip said, "No, that wouldn't be possible."

It was between late and never that Dr. Philip came to realize that his answer just didn't matter. Yes, no, I don't know? Didn't matter. This was all acted out in front of the jury who were rapt with the kabuki of the struggle (the jurors in the back row were standing up to get a better view) and saw it all for themselves. Christine was caterwauling objections from the prosecution table and Dr. Philip was giving the jury a look that Chico Marx once insightfully described as "Who you gonna believe? Me or your lying eyes?"

It was just one of those magical moments where reasonable doubt had just erupted full blown out of Zeus' head, displayed in stereo, HiDef, and in living color. I thanked Cliff for his stalwart service (he loved every moment) and then sat down. Christine then launched into full damage control in her redirect examination of Dr. Philip, asking him technical and forensic questions about point of entry, wound path, and stippling, oblivious to the reality that with each question and answer the jurors were thinking to themselves, "Hey, what are you talking about? I just saw this for myself."

Dr. Philip did the best he could. And although he didn't get any blood on any death certificates or complain about the D.A. farting on a file he was in the process of reviewing, he did get a nice letter from the County Executive thanking him for his short term service to the Office of the Medical Examiner of Onondaga County. He was sent on his way shortly after the Jeff Peterson trial ended. I don't think Fitz attended his farewell party.

Do You Believe in Magic?

The Grand Finale. The Big Windup. Game Seven. This was the chance for the D.A. to finish big in the Jeffrey Peterson case. The accepted wisdom of all trial work is that you start dramatically and end with a closing and convincing flourish if you can. Sometimes circumstances are such that you need to change the batting order or zig when you originally meant to zag. Christine was plowing straight ahead.

Although things did not seem to be going all that well for the prosecution as the Peterson case unfolded (and unraveled), it didn't seem that they ever wavered from their intention to close their proof with the most meaningful evidence they thought they had: Shaheen Bean's blood on Jeffrey Peterson's right shirt cuff. And it wasn't just the blood; it was the blood droplet stain pattern on the shirt cuff that supposedly confirmed the tale spun by Debbie Kinsey. Jeffrey Peterson had stood over the helpless Shaheen Bean and by shooting him in the head executed the guy who only seconds before was his assailant, whom he was defending himself against, but was now his helpless victim.

At least that was how it was supposed to go.

The D.A.'s blood stain pattern evidence was supposed to prove that Peterson fired the gun close enough to Bean's head so that uniquely patterned tiny droplets traveled at high velocity upwards and impacted in such a way that it described with undeniable empirical scientific accuracy that that is how the event must have happened. It dovetailed neatly into the prosecution's Truth 1. Unfortunately for the D.A., it also happened to be essentially voodoo, and wobbly voodoo at that.

Besides being burdened by its inability to explain why they were examining a long-sleeved shirt when Debbie Kinsey had the shooter wearing a short-sleeved shirt, why blood spatter would appear on Peterson's right shirt cuff and not his left if Peterson, being left-handed, would have been expected to shoot with his left hand, its inability to explain why there was no gunshot residue on Peterson and his clothing, and its inability to explain why, if he was standing over Bean as Debbie Kinsey had claimed, there was no blood on Peterson's pants or white sneakers, this theory had an additional deficiency. Even in the age of CSI, blood stain pattern evidence had, at best, a fuzzy pedigree as a forensic "science" and was still frequently legitimately criticized as a discipline only a few steps removed from junk science. A blue-ribbon Commission convened to examine the state of the forensic sciences in 2009 by the National Academy of Sciences concluded, in a universally praised Report, that "the uncertainties associated with bloodstain pattern analysis are enormous," and that experts' opinions in this discipline were generally "more subjective than scientific."

To be sure, an expert on blood stain pattern with the proper training and credentials could present a credible and compelling explanation for the presence and meaning of tiny blood droplets on all manner of surfaces, clothing, and weapons; on the other hand, a self-educated crackpot using plant misters and bedsheets in the back of his garage and calling himself an "expert" could also pontificate authoritatively on this somewhat arcane subject.

It really did come down to two things: the intrinsic and self-limiting range of what blood stain pattern evidence was actually capable of proving, and the credibility of the expert in question.

I could accept the fact that Tonto could look at a trail of the rustlers' hoofprints and tell the Lone Ranger how many horses there were and that one of the horses was lame. But when Tonto looks at the hoofprints and tells his Kemosabe that one of the bandidos must have been wearing a red flannel shirt, had a cold, and had a five-dollar bill in his pocket, Tonto belongs in the world of comic books not forensic science.

The prosecution's Tonto providing the Big Windup to their case was a lovely, educated, and quietly competent lady named Anita Zannin. She was not law enforcement, but rather an independent outside consultant. She had been an intern with and student of Dr. Herb MacDonnell, a renowned self-taught scientist engineer who was to blood stain pattern analysis as Ray Kroc was to McDonald's hamburgers. Didn't exactly invent it, but spread its forensic gospel far and wide. Ms. Zannin not only studied with Prof. MacDonnell, but she had two master's degrees and numerous certificates of seminar participation and achievement, taught a course in forensic blood stain pattern analysis at Syracuse University, and ran her own consulting business for the legal community. For all of her impressive credentials, she had never before testified as a witness, much less an expert witness.

She and Christine took the jury through an exposition of blood stain pattern analysis, its methods, scope, and history, and then, over my objection, narrated two videos demonstrating the castoff and impact blood patterns created when a bullet is shot into a blood-stained sponge. I pointed out to Judge Fahey that we were dealing with a case of homicide not spongeicide and no matter how hard a bullet strikes a sponge, it's still a sponge not a human being. He overruled my objection and let them play the videos.

Over the course of two hours, Christine had Ms. Zannin, provide her guided tour and commentary on most of the nearly 200 exhibits the prosecution had offered into evidence. (Not to be outdone in the more-is-better department, I had loaded the trial record with 55 of my own.) She particularly dwelt on the purple and white checked shirt which had been studied, photographed, and analyzed as if it was the Shroud of Turin. The jury was interested in this at first; but after an hour or two, it became clear to everyone except Christine and Ms. Zannin that we had wandered into too-much-information-land and attentions started to lag.

We eventually got around to why Anita Zannin was there: based upon her review of the evidence and her analysis of the blood stain patterns she was able to examine and analyze, what was her opinion on the following subject?

Q. Based on your training and your experience and all of the materials that you have reviewed, to a reasonable degree of scientific certainty, were you able to form an opinion as to the position the person who was wearing the shirt was in when the back spatter was deposited on the shirt?

A. I believe the most likely position the wearer of the shirt would have been in would have been a standing, stooping position.

As far as I was concerned, we had now ventured into Tonto comic book land and this answer was not going to stand. It is for this very reason the gods of trial work invented cross-examination.

The Peterson trial had attracted unusually full galleries for its two-week limited run, and when I began my cross-examination of Anita Zannin I noticed that the spectator count in the courtroom was at near capacity. Naturally, I instinctively attributed this to my own personal star quality and vainly indulged the thought that people had come far and wide to witness the brilliance with which I was to set aflame the wreckage of what was left to the prosecution's case on this, the last day of the D.A.'s proof. Not quite Bunky.

In addition to the Peterson and Bean families, there were the usual clutch of young defense lawyers and assistant D.A.'s who daily monitored the trial and even the odd judge or two (even though for some strange reason judges weren't supposed to sit in on their colleagues' trials). The largest contingent, by far, however, were the cops from the Syracuse Police Department, its lab, its evidence recovery team, and their administration. They were not there rooting for me, but they weren't there to show the flag in support of the D.A. either. In the main, they were there to see what it was that compelled Bill Fitzpatrick and his crew to go outside the Department, to see who could opine and explain better than them what all of the physical evidence they had worked hard to collect meant, and to judge for themselves whether this expert was so much better than they were that the County taxpayers' money had to be spent to bring her into the case. They took a particular burn to the fact that she had not consulted with them at all. These were not happy campers and to the extent I could somewhat mollify their unhappiness by diminishing Anita Zannin's expertise through a vigorous cross-examination, they would be more than OK with that. They came to watch.

I pretty much knew where I wanted to take my cross-examination of Anita Zannin and I had planned accordingly, making a detailed outline of my questions and the topics I wanted to cover. Although she hadn't testified before the Grand Jury, she did compile a detailed report, something which the law required the D.A. to provide to me ahead of the trial. So, I knew well in advance what her investigative method and approach had been and what she was going to say when she testified. My approach was to be respectful and deferential up to a point. But only up to a point. I thought her conclusion and opinion on how the shooting must have happened was simply unsupportable nonsense and my objective was to demonstrate that without either attacking her professionally or making her look foolish. She turned out to be a wily witness, fully capable of holding her own.

My main line of attack was predicated on the inevitably subjective nature of all expert opinions when it came to blood stain pattern evidence. I wanted the jury to recognize that although blood stain pattern analysis called itself a "forensic science," it wasn't really a science at all. Early on, I got her to acknowledge the National Academy of Sciences findings that "the uncertainties associated with bloodstain pattern analysis are enormous," and that experts' opinions in this discipline were generally "more subjective than scientific."

She conceded that. Of course, she had no choice since the Report of the National Academy of Science, which she recognized as critically important and widely influential, said exactly that. I then started reminding her (and the jury) that each time the D.A. asked for her opinion it was couched in terms of scientific certainty. The language of these kinds of questions posed to expert witnesses are rote and formulaic and every good lawyer is careful to phrase his or her question of this kind in the following way: "Doctor, do you have an opinion within a reasonable degree of medical certainty...?" or "Professor, do you have an opinion within a reasonable degree of scientific certainty...?" Jurors usually don't pay close attention to precisely how these kinds of questions are posed; but judges do and so do lawyers. And to be admissible, an opinion must be proffered in that kind of precise way. Christine knew that and she did that. Over and over. So often, in fact, that it invited the jury to believe that they were hearing scientific opinions. They were no such thing and the overall intention of my cross-examination was to debunk such a notion.

So I was working my way towards trying to peel back the patina of "scientific" respectability, to show that what she was really espousing was a subjective opinion, one which was resting on a very wobbly set of facts that the jury well knew (no blood on the pants and sneakers, no gunshot residue, right cuff of a left handed person, long sleeve/short sleeve). So I asked her the following question:

Q. So that with respect to the litany of questions that you answered in the last half-hour or so with respect to do you have an opinion within a reasonable degree of scientific certainty, whatever that opinion was is not an opinion based on science is it?

A. Not on one of the four pure sciences, no.

Okay, I'm satisfied by that answer so far. She's conceding that it's not a "pure" science, but she's hedging.

My planned follow-up was to get her to concede the very subjective nature of this enterprise, that there is little empirical certainty to it, and that because there are so many variables, what she was doing was essentially just guessing:

Q. It is, would you agree with me, that blood stain and blood spatter analysis is as much an art as it is a science?

A. I don't know that I would say art.

She's being wary of me, reluctant to make the concession she knows I want her to make. So, violating the first law of cross-examination, I foolishly ask her an open-ended question, one that I don't already know the answer to. I ask her to define it for me. And she knocks it out of the park with a jackpot answer:

Q. Let's get on the same page. If it's not a science and it's not an art, what is it?

A. It's a discipline based on scientific principles.

This witness was one smart lady. She knew full well that my objective was to show that blood stain pattern analysis was not a "science" at all and that in many cases, this case especially, it was not much more than a good guess. As meticulously as I had prepared for my cross-examination of her, I have to confess that I was momentarily set back on my heels. I simply didn't expect an answer like that. I paused for a moment, fully aware that the full gallery was closely following our back and forth, particularly the coppers in the back row who were practically keeping a box score.

And then, a moment of inspiration. The question just came to me:

Q. Is magic, magic a science?

A. No.

Q. It's based upon scientific principles of perception and speed is it not?

A. Sure.

Q. Would you agree with that?

A. Sure.

Q. It's based on scientific principles where the observer is deceived into seeing something that in fact is not there, but it's the scientific principles at work of perception, vision, speed, distraction, isn't that all true?

A. That's true

The coppers in the back row loved it.

It was an important moment and it came at an important point of the trial. I wanted to just turn to the jury then and there and announce, "See? They've been trying to fool you. She doesn't know any more or better than anyone else. It's a guess. It's just voodoo." Of course, the rules say you can't do that. But I didn't have to. I glanced over at them and by the look on their faces I knew that they had sent Ms. Zannin off to Tonto-land.

After eight days of proof, the prosecution rested. It was time to bring the show to a close.

Summing Up

This could be the part of the story where I tell you what a barn burner of a summation I gave, how I knocked it out of the park, took no prisoners, and singlehandedly won an acquittal for my client. I could tell you in detail of my soaring and emotional rhetoric about self-defense, protecting yourself, protecting your loved one. This could be the part where I tell you that I said to the jury "If their case was a car, would you buy it? I don't think that you'd even drive it." I'd love to go over all that again in detail. No point. Forget self-defense, the Castle Defense, forensic ballistics, the dentist on the courtroom floor, or blood spatter magic evidence. It all really didn't matter.

The jury finally had the case and there was nothing more to be done.

Waiting for a verdict in a criminal trial, especially one which has gone on for days and drained every effort and emotion you have, is like waiting for a loved one to come out of major surgery. You experience a total loss of control (a foreign emotion for trial lawyers) and feel a deep fear that something has gone wrong and you can't do anything about it. You sit in the hallway, your mind a blank except for the niggling echoes of things you forgot to say in summation. Sometimes it's hours, it can even continue over excruciating days. Sometimes the jury will send out a note and everyone huddles and strains to read the tea leaves, hoping there's a signal from that small ship in a storm-tossed sea. And then. A note. "We have reached a verdict."

Then there is a dreadful suddenness The Judge asks the foreperson if the Jury has reached a verdict, they say yes, and, in a matter of less than a minute, the rest of your client's life is fatefully pronounced and dictated. Guilty, Not Guilty; on an existential level it really doesn't matter. No one accused of a serious crime ever recovers from going through the experience, the profound peril you have faced, your willingness to trust in other people.

As things turned out, instead of my brilliant summation, I could have read the Betty Crocker recipe for orange- glazed chicken with broccoli and mashed potatoes and the jury would have come to the same conclusion. Not Guilty.

The prosecution called 19 witnesses and introduced more than 100 exhibits over the nine days of trial. Despite the huffing, puffing, shapeshifting, and blustering, the reality was that the prosecution never had a case to begin with. This reality was lost on Christine, Sal, Melinda McGunnigle, Fitz, and me, a consequence of all of us spending too much time in law school. From jump street, the Jury simply didn't see this as a murder. They took less than two hours to deliberate and acquit Jeffrey Peterson. And that included lunch. I don't know if they had the orange-glazed chicken.

For me, I was happy for Jeffrey Peterson and his family. He shook my hand and said thank you and I did the same with him. Then I gathered my files, my papers and notes, the exhibits I'd never need or use again, and left the courthouse with Sal, in search of another case of yet unchallenged injustice.

OTHER PEOPLE'S MONEY

Several years ago, the Chief Judge of the Federal District Court asked me to participate in an orientation program for newly admitted attorneys. I was to be a panelist and each of us was to speak on a different topic of importance and interest. My assigned topic was the Criminal Justice Act, the Federal program which is designed to provide the assistance of counsel to accused persons who could not afford to hire their own attorney. The CJA program does important work and given what's at stake, it's really critical that CJA attorneys who enroll in the service (which pays a reasonable if not overly generous fee) know what they're doing and be committed to the work. I was given 10 minutes.

Most people who know me know that I am barely capable of clearing my throat in 10 minutes. Nevertheless, I welcomed the opportunity to address a roomful of newbies and see if I could motivate them to get involved in the CJA program.

The assigned title for my talk was "CJA Work in the Northern District: Doing Your Part for Justice in Your Community." Catchy enough, I thought, and it gave me the opportunity to cover a lot of ground. But, still, I only had 10 minutes. So I created what I thought was a nifty if not comprehensive Power Point overview of what the program does and how you qualify for it, adding in some nuts and bolts practical advice, and even a witty cartoon or two. And to be sure that I didn't forget any of the points I wanted to make, I printed out the Power Point presentation.

I'm sitting there waiting my turn and sitting next to me is Magistrate Judge Gustave J. DiBianco, a laconic and witty guy who, thank goodness, took his job seriously. Gus looks over at the table and sees my printed Power Point presentation and the title page which reads "CJA Work in the Northern District: Doing Your Part for Justice in Your Community." Below it, I added a quotation: "The only law that matters is criminal law; everything else is just about other people's money."

Gus looks at me and points to the quote and says, "That's a great quote. Who said that?"

I said, "I did.

JUSTIN CASE, MEET GENERAL NORIEGA

Y ou never know where your next lesson in the law will come from or who will teach it to you. I got a valuable lesson once from a guy I represented named Greg. I can't really remember the details of how he came to be my client, but I have a vague recollection that his stepfather was a retired judge and maybe the word of mouth highway led Greg to my door. I'm just not sure about that. What I am sure of was that Greg was in very deep shit and he was indicted in a large-scale cocaine conspiracy, one of the counts being an A-II felony which carried with it a mandatory life sentence with a minimum of 8 years. That definitely had my attention; Greg's? well, not so much.

Greg was absolutely convinced that the prosecution had no case against him and that he also had the greatest lawyer in the world, namely me. I will confess that there are few people in the history of mankind who have had a higher opinion of me than me, but even my inflated sense of my own skill set never really unmoored me from reality and a set of unfortunate facts. And Greg's enthusiasm over how I was going to kick the prosecutor's ass all around was just a tad destabilizing, especially since early in the case I was convinced that Greg was going down. Still, though, and Greg's delirious

96

idolatry aside, there was something in the case to talk about.

Here's the basic scenario: a bunch of guys are having cocaine mailed to them from Florida. The packages are being delivered to a copy shop one of the guys owns. The return address is a non-existent street in Ft. Lauderdale and the sender is "Justin Case." Greg thought the Justin Case nom de drogo was really cool and he couldn't get over himself for thinking it up. Well, notwithstanding the fact that the police had conducted surveillance, mail covers (where they get to open packages before they arrive, even the ones that look like they have been sent from Aunt Tillie's Strawberry Jam Factory), and wiretapping, they could never develop any hard evidence that Greg was the actual supplier. All they really had was a mope named Frank who owned the copy shop and was supposedly the only one who knew where the cocaine was coming from.

Frank, of course, had flipped on everyone else, including Greg, but the rest of this crew were active enough on their own to have supplied the police with plenty of evidence of their drug dealing complicity. Frank claimed to have had phone conversations with Greg (no tapes), sent him money (cash by mail of course), and taken at least one personal delivery from Greg (unwitnessed, never surveilled). So the case against Greg came down to Frank's word which, to be frank, wasn't very good. His cred suffered from just a tad too many prior criminal convictions, one of which was that special Godsend to attorneys tasked to cross- examine informants like Frank: a perjury conviction.

Notwithstanding Greg's nearly irrational enthusiasm for our defense, I had my doubts, particularly because if we lost I would get to go back to my office disappointed for the afternoon, but Greg would have a one-way ticket to never-coming-back land.

So it's Friday afternoon and the trial is set for Monday. I'm trying to get Greg to focus on reality and he's not just doubtful, he's obstinately resistant. He's simply intoxicated with the thought that his brilliant lawyer is going to destroy Frank and lead the parade out of court and back onto the beaches of Ft. Lauderdale. No one likes flattery more than me, but he's wearing me down.

Without asking him, I pick up the phone and call the prosecutor, Terry Kelly, a laconic, likeable, and good-natured fellow who seemed to have graduated law school tired and never really woke up. Terry liked the idea of getting a paycheck every two weeks whether he won any particular trial or not. His idea of working as a prosecutor in the criminal justice system was that basically it was a matter of moving inventory around the factory floor. You lose a box here or there, you can still count on a new supply coming into the loading dock out back.

Terry's offer had been 8 to Life, the then-minimum sentence for an A-II drug felony. After a brief back and forth, I get him to agree to lower the charge to an A-III and 6 to Life. "Life" in these type of drug cases is, by the way, a palliative fiction designed to make the public happy.

You don't really get Life unless you are El Chapo or The Unabomber. The convicted defendant does his minimum sentence in jail and then is loosed upon the parole system which, in theory, is supposed to track these miscreants for the rest of their lives. Given the workload of most parole officers, who spend a lot of time in their cubicles moving around their own boxes of inventory, "lifetime supervision" morphs into something like a five year stretch of checking in once in a while. And then, if the parole officer is really lucky, the parolee gets discharged from parole because he's not much more than a lingering nuisance, or he reoffends, goes back to jail, and then becomes somebody else's problem.

Terry's at 6 to Life. The rock-bottom minimum on an A-III is 3 to Life, so I keep at him. He finally says, as I knew he would, if the Judge wants to give Greg 3 to Life he won't make an issue out of it (at that point he's probably got one eye on the loading dock out back with a forklift beep-beep-beeping and with a pallet of new inventory arriving).

The next call is a little harder. The trial judge is Judge Burke, a man who takes his job seriously and has an Irishman's sense of justice (which is sometimes a very good thing, other times a painful experience). I admire him very much and he is very fond of me. But he's not in the habit of doing my clients any favors just because I'm one of his boys. And I know better than to be flippant with him when discussing the disposition of a drug case.

But he's also got his own inventory concerns and he's going to at least listen if he's told that both the prosecution and defense are OK with a plea and a fixed sentence. Unless, of course, there's some factor of outrage or real harm connected with the case. Mercifully, and despite the seriousness of the consequences for Greg, Judge Burke hasn't heard anything about Justin Case, Ft. Lauderdale, Frank the Snitch, or much else about the matter. To him, it's an A-II drug case. OK, maybe an A-III. But, still, it's inventory.

So, he hears me out. I tell him Terry "doesn't have a problem" with an A-III and 3 to Life. Long pause. He finally says, "OK, but the guy's gotta plead on Monday. I got other things to do." At this point, he's also looking over to his own loading dock and knows that he can set up another trial for Monday even though this is Friday afternoon. I tell him I'll call him back.

Now, all of this is happening while Greg is sitting on the other side of my desk. He's giving himself a manicure. No kidding. He's been sort of listening, seemingly as unconcerned as if I was ordering Chinese takeout.

"Greg, I got them down to 3 to Life. You just heard it. You should take it. We're out of time. You gotta decide now"

"I dunno Eddie. You can win this case for me."

"Greg, I just did."

"I dunno."

We sit in silence for a minute or two. I look over to the corner of my desk. The new issue of Newsweek is laying there and on the cover is the utterly remarkable booking photo of Manuel Noriega holding a jail card against his chest with the date and booking number splayed across the foreground in bold white letters.

I pick it up and show it to Greg.

"See this guy? He was the President of Panama moving cocaine by the ton. They got him. Does this suggest anything to you?"

Greg gives it a thoughtful look. "Yeah, prices are gonna go up."

Monday comes. Greg pleads to the deal. He gets 3 to Life. He goes to jail. But that's not the end of the story.

Now it's 18 months later. In the morning mail, along with Newsweek and that month's telephone bill, comes a letter from Greg. It's handwritten front and back on yellow legal paper and my first reaction is that Greg is filling out some downtime in the Attica prison library by catching me up. Catching me up he is doing. But it's not from the Attica Correctional Facility in western New York where he was supposed to be because Judge Burke had sent him there. It's from the Miami Dade Metropolitan Jail.

Greg starts out by singing his usual love song to me, telling me how I'm the greatest lawyer in human history and how I saved his life. I'm starting to think is this guy mentally ill? Maybe he's gay and is in love with me? How could doing 3 to Life be such a really great result? I read on. And learn more than a thing or two about clients, myself, and what I sometimes miss about the Big Picture.

What I definitely learned was that Greg was a whole lot smarter than I ever gave him credit for and that the manicure he was giving himself on the other side of my desk while I was working the phones struggling to get him a better plea deal was just his way of letting this particular interruption in his Grand Plan sort of work itself out anyway it could.

Unbeknownst to me (and to Terry Kelly and Judge Burke), Greg had been an active informant for the DEA for years and whilst this silly minor sideshow was resolving itself in Syracuse, New York, the Feds in Miami had major plans for Greg's cooperation in a largescale trafficking case. So after we go through the kabuki play in Judge Burke's courtroom and Greg is unceremoniously whisked away to Attica, he sits there pretty much in reception for about a week until the Florida Feds show up with a Federal Writ. Greg is then flown – in a private jet – down to Miami, where he is thereafter sequestered in a private hotel room, an accommodation which had little resemblance to or connection with his initially proposed lodging in a cell in the Attica Correctional

Facility.

The South Florida trial goes on for 15 months and Greg is ordering room service most of that time. I really have no idea what the case was about; it just seems to me that when your witness is stashed in a hotel ordering shrimp cocktails and sorbet for a really extended period of time, the case is Big and the witness is Important.

The trial in Florida comes to an end and it's time to check out of the hotel. But then Greg reveals to the Feds that he also has bigger and better information on something else (Greg's got his own inventory to move around.) The Feds are interested but not convinced. Instead of returning him to Attica to serve out the rest of his New York sentence (that clock has been running ever since they took him down to the Florida sun) they stick him in the Metropolitan Detention Center in Miami.

At this point, of course, Greg has been outed as a major informant so it's the Special Housing Unit for him (no more room service, thinner mattress). He whiles away the time writing letters (like the one to me), playing basketball in the limited rec time he's given, and eating the Oreo cookies his mother sends him on a weekly basis. Greg's mother has been a hovering presence in his life, and she tries to keep up both his spirits and hers by writing him supportive notes and sending ample supplies of the Oreos.

Greg's cookie stash gets the attention of one of the other inmates who is allowed to play b-ball with him in the Special Housing Unit. Turns out this guy craves Oreos and when he was the President of Panama he too had a nearly endless supply on hand.

Greg is sharp enough to realize that my reaction to this

story would be incredulity (I've had enough years of practicing criminal law to hone my bullshit detector skills to the Grandmaster Level), so he tears off a page from the sports section of a Spanish language newspaper with a story about Steffi Graff playing tennis and has the Generalissimo sign it "Too Ed, Noriega!" Greg writes to tell me that he has informed 'Manny" that if Roy Black (the celebrated Miami criminal defense attorney who was representing Noriega) lets him down, I'm the guy he should call. (Never did hear from the Generalissimo.)

I learned two important and valuable things from representing Greg: some clients are actually smarter than me and have their own definition of what's a successful outcome. And Manuel Noriega likes Oreo cookies.

CAPTAIN MITCH'S INDEPENDENCE DAY & THE BIG LITTLE GALLOO SHOOTOUT

Americans like to celebrate Independence Day with a bang. You couldn't find anybody more American than Captain Mitch.

A short gray-haired man in his early fifties, Mitch had the chiseled good looks of a western cowboy, the rough hands of a commercial fisherman (which he was), and a body that could best be described as a beer keg balanced on two short bowed legs. His arms were well muscled from years of working as a charter boat captain on Lake Ontario, and when he wasn't using them to haul in lines or to push heavy equipment around the deck, they crossed neatly into themselves when Captain Mitch folded his arms. When listening to you, his favored inclination was to cross them over his broad chest, signaling that, yeah, he got what you were saying, but it wasn't likely that he was going to be changing his mind anytime soon. In this or the next lifetime.

Despite his mostly justifiable sense of self-sufficiency, Captain Mitch knew his own limits and was willing to look for help if he really needed it. In this case, he really needed it.

He sat across from my desk with his default pose of folded arms. Sitting in a lawyer's office was pretty low on

Captain Mitch's list of priorities, but when he pulled out the Grand Jury subpoena from his back pocket, his needs became fairly clear fairly quickly. Generally speaking, nobody told Captain Mitch what to do and he took a particular burn to the idea that the Federal Government was looming large in his rear-view mirror in an attempt to make him say what he didn't want to say. Well, that's not exactly true. Captain Mitch did want to talk about it, just not to the Government. His main question, understandably, was Do I have to go? And then, If I do, do I really have to testify?

I explained to Captain Mitch the ways of prosecutors and Grand Juries. There are 23 pretty average citizens sitting in something resembling an oversized classroom. Nobody knows who they are outside of that room and all they really have to do is listen and do what they are told. The teacher for the day (this person is called a prosecutor) addresses them in large block capital letters and tells them that they will be listening to a parade of witnesses to spell out, in the most general terms possible, what may or may not have been a crime. (Wink, wink. It almost always turns out to be a crime.)

The Grand Jury is actually an arm of the Court and when you get a Grand Jury subpoena it's a whole lot more than a note to go the principal's office. It's a Court Order. You could, of course, take the 5th and refuse to testify, but prosecutors have a work around for that. They can march you in front of a Judge who will then grant you immunity, but that kind of immunity – it's called "use immunity" – only means that they can't use what you say against you; anybody else that you are asked about is fair game. And if they have other evidence that incriminates you, "use immunity" would be as useful as a paper umbrella in a windstorm.

So, what was it that Captain Mitch didn't want to tell the Government?

Captain Mitch was a stalwart member of the charter boat fraternity in Henderson Harbor, a small fishing village nestled in the nub of a small promontory jutting into eastern Lake Ontario. It was a lovely, small, and quaint village of maybe 1,500 permanent residents but the population swelled during the spring and summer months when the fishing for lake trout, bass, walleye, and good-sized salmon attracted anglers from great distances. The salmon fishing, in particular, used to be really spectacular until the construction of the mammoth Nine Mile Point nuclear power plant a few miles south of the harbor. The salmon were still fairly abundant but unless your tastes ran to large slices of lox that glowed in the dark, you fished for the good-sized salmon mainly for the thrill of hauling in a twenty pound scaled creature to flop around on the boat's deck before taking a picture and tossing it back.

Nine Mile had put a major crimp in the charter boat business for sure but the captains were resigned to the march of nuclear energy progress and instead they turned to other game fish, mainly bass, a species which were plentiful and provided plenty of fight and fun for the charter clients.

And Then the Cormorants Showed Up.

Now unless you are a lifetime member of the National Audubon Society and also have a deep fascination for ornithological curiosities, a cormorant can be regarded as an ungainly and unattractive creature who only has two purposes in life: catching and eating fish in enormous quantities and making baby cormorants. They have long and very narrow snake-like necks upon which are perched narrow fuzzy feathered skulls with long dagger-like hooked beaks. Their serpentine head and neck are affixed to a clumsy body and a pair of powerful webbed feet which can propel them to remarkable depths of over 100 feet. They are not much in the flying department, but they can dive for fish like nobody's business.

For centuries, fishermen in Japan tied long lines to the cormorants' feet and fitted rings around their necks so that they couldn't swallow the larger fish that they snagged after diving. The fishermen would then let the bird dive, gobble its fill, and surface with the catch of the day. How the Japanese fishermen retrieved the bigger fish from the cormorant's gullet is information I would suppose neither you nor I really need. Just know that they did. The birds are just fish-eating machines.

Another thing about Captain Mitch's story that you need to know is that cormorants are migratory water birds. As such, they are protected by the Federal Migratory Bird Treaty Act. They, of course, are too concerned with eating fish to know this, so they mindlessly move from place to place in great numbers in order to wipe out fish populations across the United States and Canada. There are a few pockets inside the USA which are inhospitable to these creatures; since catfish farming (no kidding) is big business in Arkansas and Louisiana you can legally shoot a cormorant on sight if you are a licensed catfish farmer. (Please don't ask how you get one of these licenses; suffice to say that catfish farming is not big business in New York State.)

In any case, Captain Mitch, who this story is supposed to be about, couldn't care less about catfish farming. What he cared about, in a major way, was that cormorants were eating the heart out of his business. They descended upon Henderson Harbor like a biblical pestilence and what really infuriated Captain Mitch and his fellow charter captains was that despite their protestations, the Government didn't seem all that interested in doing anything about it. Bad enough they had to put up with a nuclear power plant in their backyard. Now their livelihood was being literally eaten away by swarms of prehistoric looking birds who were being protected for God knows what reason but eating and procreating like a sky full of African locusts. Enough was e-fucking nuff.

The cormorants around Henderson settled five miles offshore on Little Galloo island, a completely undistinguished 55-acre rock pile consisting mainly of boulders, driftwood, and guano. (It once had trees and grass, but the cormorants took care of that; they decimated the place to make room for breeding space.) The birds gathered in breeding pairs, numbering in total maybe a thousand or two at any given time. Given that in a typical year cormorants consumed an estimated 87 million, that's million, fish from the waters of Eastern Lake Ontario, their presence on Little Galloo was not a welcome sight to Captain Mitch or his mates.

What was particularly infuriating was that when they were not fishing or reproducing, the cormorants perched on rocks or driftwood and splayed their long wings out sideways while stretching their necks vertically, and then holding the pose long enough for you to imagine that they were showing off what at least they thought was not only the beauty of their bodies to other cormorants but their awareness that some law written and passed by pointy-headed Congressmen protected them from harm. What they were actually doing was drying off their feathers. But any reasonable person could think that what they were really doing was flouting their invulnerability, being a protected species and all.

The charter boat captains hated these birds with a nearly unbound fury and protested in every venue they could: the DEC (Department of Environmental Conservation), the Governor, their state senator, their congressman. No help. And because the charter fishing business was suffering so badly, the captains had the entire community behind them since, after all, tourism was about the only source of revenue for the folks in Henderson Harbor. What they got back was a lot of yadda, even when they came up with at least one common sense solution: sending a group of boy scouts onto Little Galloo with a shitload of baby oil to coat every cormorant egg they could find. The oil would clog the pores of the eggshells which in turn would bring about the early demise of these not yet federally protected birds to be. No go. Wouldn't work. Too many clearances needed to make it happen. Made too much sense to the Gummint.

It got to the point that the captains went to a silk-screening company to produce hundreds of black tee shirts with the image of a cormorant centered in a red target circle with a sideways slash running across the image. The tee shirts were sold to fund the captains' efforts to lobby DEC officials, futile as those efforts were turning out to be. The tee shirts were a big hit around the Harbor. Hundreds were sold and you saw them everywhere. Any person with a shred of common sense should have seen what was coming. The Gummint being the Gummint, of course, didn't.

What was coming was the Fourth of July. In Sackets Harbor.

The Big Bang

The village of Sackets Harbor lies just a few miles north of Henderson along the Ontario shoreline. It is somewhat larger than Henderson Harbor, but it still retains the touristy feel of a waterfront community, with quaint shops, several marinas, a lighthouse, and periodic Revolutionary War re-enactments. It goes big on the Fourth of July. People pour in from the neighboring communities to enjoy harborside concerts, games of frisbee, grilled burgers and hot dogs, and, in the evening, a pretty large and impressive fireworks display. The fireworks can be seen and heard from many miles away. In fact, even though Little Galloo Island is squatting silently in the darkness out on the water some eight miles distant, you can see and hear Sacket's all-American Big Bang from there as well as from Henderson Harbor itself.

On this particular Fourth of July night, Captain Mitch was not interested in hot dogs, frisbees, or concerts. While many of his neighbors in and around Henderson Harbor happily trundled their picnic baskets up to Sackets to enjoy the festivities, Captain Mitch was quietly meeting up dockside with a small and select platoon of other charter boat captains. Each of them had their own fireworks show in mind that night, one that they had been planning for a long time.

There were eight in all, launching in three boats. And in place of their usual supplies of minnows, bait fish, crabs, and worms, they had an ample store of shotguns and birdshot. Very ample. This small flotilla of determined men slid silently out of the Harbor on a night of no moon and fireworks in the distance. They were about to strike their own blows for free enterprise, and although their declarations of liberty from governmental interference may not have been quite on the scale of Sam Adams leading the Sons of Liberty on their Tea Party protests in the Boston Harbor, they meant serious business and wanted to let it be known they were done asking.

The three boats quietly trolled up to Little Galloo, killing their lights when they were about 100 yards offshore. The ammonia stench from the cormorants' guano confirmed they were in the right place for sure. The distant fireworks from Sackets Harbor rumbled and flashed in the night sky.

Three of the men got into a small Zodiac inflatable with a 15 hp trolling motor and went straight ashore, causing a squawk and squabble amongst the couple of dozen cormorants resting along the shoreline. More squawking and caterwauling when the men activated their headlamps. They each had a shotgun and a long pole to stir up the birds. The three boats had floated nearer the island but were neatly and safely triangulated with each other to maximize the shooting angle for the fleeing birds.

With the lethal precision of Seal Team 6 taking out Osama bin Laden, the three men on the island unleashed their firepower and waved their sticks and the cormorants rose as a great flock in the night sky, with a cacophony of caws and a swoosh like a legion of bats rushing out of the mouth of a great cave. Once the birds were airborne, which didn't take long, the boat lights suddenly came on full and the men aboard, all charter captains whose livelihood was being sapped away by these voracious creatures, blasted and blasted and blasted until their supply of birdshot was gone.

The island's stench of guano was quickly overwhelmed by the miasma of sulphur and gun smoke that hovered over the lake's waters. There was a lot of shooting. But it was over rather quickly and even though the captains' volleys in concert were deafening, anyone on shore around the village who might possibly have heard it would have naturally assumed it was part of the Sackets Harbor fireworks display.

Daylight brought a ghastly sight. There were dead birds everywhere, over a thousand of them, on the island, lolling limply in the small waves washing up on Little Galloo, and floating all around in a multitude of scattered small bloody bundles offshore. The dozens of flightless hatchlings and fledglings were left squawking in the grips of what was unquestionably some exotic form of avian PTSD. It was, in short, a wide scale mess.

A group of boaters out for a day cruise came upon the carnage and called it in to the Coast Guard Power Squadron for Lake Ontario; they in turn contacted the New York State Police and the Mounties (yes! the Mounties! Little Galloo is spitting distance from Canada) and then the DEC, the EPA, the FBI and then the U.S. Attorney.

The Gummint rapidly got its collective shorts in a major twist in a major hurry. Which, more or less, is what Captain Mitch and his buds very much intended. From their point of view, they just got tired of asking and got equally tired of being told that these agencies were studying the problem. As far as Captain Mitch was concerned: well, "fucking study this, assholes."

As you might expect, the story of the Little Galloo shootout went viral. And this was even before the advent of Twitter, Facebook, and WhatsApp. It was all over the papers (and I'm not talking the Henderson Harbor Pennysaver here), picked up by the Associated Press, and got national television exposure. Nothing like a thousand dead birds to stir the passions of PETA, National Geographic, and the National Association of Self-important Buttinskies.

One source of special concern, as you might expect, was the DEC. A small army of their investigators and forensic specialists descended on the Harbor. The townspeople were happy to see them. After all, these guys needed to eat, rent rooms, and buy tee shirts (especially the black ones with cormorants situated in a target field on them). The investigators did what investigators do: they investigated. But for all their knocking on doors and polite inquiries, they largely got nowhere. Everybody in town had their "suspicions."

In truth, of course, they all knew who did it (you'd have to be a low-grade moron not to know it was the captains), but they didn't really know. In any case, nobody was anxious to give up the captains and there continued to be a lingering resentment directed towards the DEC. Where the hell were you guys when the fishing around here went in the crapper because of these ugly birds?

Even though the cleanup of the dead birds was a major undertaking, the investigation into who was responsible went nowhere. This particularly displeased Assistant United States Attorney Craig Benedict, a short, terrier-like individual, a former college wrestler with the personality that goes with that recreation, and someone who gave new meaning to the word zealotry. Some lawyers get their way through disarming their adversaries with good humor and charm. Not Craig. His narrow-focus determination to prosecute any and all environmental crimes (of whatever scale, relevance, or importance) didn't earn him many fans in the defense bar. In truth, because he regarded himself as his own autonomous crusader within the U.S. Attorney's Office, he didn't have a whole lot of admirers in his own office either. Every offense, no matter how minor, generated a breathless reaction.

Craig was utterly stunned that the transgression was not deserving of frontpage treatment by the *New York Times*. Above the fold. His favorite tactic was to attempt to steamroller the defense and then demand that the final disposition include an agreement that the defense not engage in any "end zone dances." This was a reflection not only of his own win at all costs attitude but of his own basic insecurity. Many defense attorneys simply turned away cases where he was the prosecutor. Perhaps cowardly, perhaps not in the finest traditions of the defense bar, but countervailed by the age-old aphorism that life was too short.

It was hard to say what infuriated Craig more: the wholesale slaughter of more than a thousand cormorants or the silence of the people of Henderson Harbor who were reluctant to give up the perpetrators. Everybody knew it was the captains. Craig knew it was the captains. He just couldn't make a case with cooperating witnesses because there weren't any.

Undeterred by the mere technicality of having no evidence, Craig decided to force the issue by drawing up a Grand Jury subpoena. As the Kalashnikov is to terrorists, a Grand Jury subpoena is to prosecutors: frightening, powerful, and gets the job done. A Grand Jury subpoena is essentially a Court Order to testify; disobedience will land you in jail. If the wusses of Henderson weren't going to talk to his investigators, they damn well would be giving it up to a Grand Jury. Astutely figuring out that even if he hauled in a basketful of townspeople, they could and would truthfully say that they really didn't "know" (which, taken literally, was true), Craig sat down at his word processor, pulled up a blank template form entitled "Grand Jury Subpoena," and typed in the name of the first person he was sure did know: Captain Mitch.

There was no question that Craig's outrage over the cormorant shooting inflamed his usual mode of zealotry and it would have been a fool's errand to try and talk him out of it. On the other hand, anyone who even vaguely knew Captain Mitch knew that Grand Jury Subpoena or not, nobody was going to make him give up his fellow boat captains, least of all to the Government. But, yet, there was this additional wild card: Mitch, the captains, and pretty much everybody else in Henderson wanted the Government to know it was them, wanted the Government to know that this was bigger and more important than some bullshit Migratory Bird Act misdemeanor violation, wanted them to know that these were citizens standing up to preserve their livelihood. They weren't criminals, they were patriots.

So, a Federal EPA investigator showed up at Captain Mitch's bungalow and dropped a Grand Jury subpoena off for him. Literally dropped it off. Captain Mitch knew who the guy was and knew what the piece of paper in his hand was too; he just wasn't going to accept it. So the EPA guy dropped it at Mitch's feet and got back in his car to drive off.

Which brings us back to Captain Mitch sitting in my office listening to my seminar about Grand Juries.

Irresistible Force Meets Immovable Object

Here's the thing: Mitch was OK with the Government knowing it was him; he was proud of it. On the other hand, he would be goddamned if he was forced to name names and give up his friends. Just wasn't gonna happen.

So, on the appointed day and hour, Captain Mitch and I trundle off to the Federal Building. Usually these kinds of proceedings are preceded by a little "meet and greet" in a small room off of the Grand Jury room. The prosecutor introduces himself or herself, tells the witness what is in store and what questions will be asked, and says they are available to respond to any concerns before they go inside to the Grand Jury (where lawyers for the witness are not allowed). Mitch just sat there, with his arms folded of course, not saying much of anything. His body and face, on the other hand, are unmistakably radiating "nofuckinway." As obstinate and stiff-necked as Craig himself could be, he readily recognized the same attitude in Captain Mitch's stare back at him. Craig asked me if I had explained immunity, contempt, and the 5th Amendment to my client. Insulting as that was, I just said "He's taking the 5th Craig."

Without further ceremony or conversation, Craig got up and said, "Let's go." Captain Mitch glared at him, looked at me, got up and disappeared with Craig behind the door of the Grand Jury. I wasn't witness to what happened next but given the fact that they came out in tandem within five minutes after they went in, it wasn't hard to conjure it all up.

In fact, it went pretty much as advertised. Craig asked Captain Mitch his name, Captain Mitch answered. Craig asked Captain Mitch his address, Captain Mitch answered. The rest, as they say, was silence. Except for the part where Captain Mitch told Craig to go fuck himself. Which, although heartfelt, was not a good idea; it wasn't exactly the way I had advised him to assert his right to remain silent under the 5th Amendment of the United States Constitution.

to the 3rd Floor

The Grand Jury meets on the 8th floor of the Federal Building. The next venue, and the one Craig had in mind, as I expected, was on the 3rd floor. That would be the courtroom of Senior United States District Court Judge Howard G. Munson. So we go to Munson's courtroom and he listens patiently to Craig's laying out the details of Captain Mitch's refusal to answer questions after being subpoenaed to appear before the Grand Jury. To Craig's great credit (which somewhat surprised me), he left off the go fuck yourself part. Craig wanted Munson to order Captain Mitch to testify under penalty of contempt.

Under the law, in exchange for Captain Mitch's giving up his 5th A. rights, Munson would grant Captain Mitch limited "use immunity." Since I had previously explained to Captain Mitch that if the Judge granted him "use immunity" he would no longer have any 5th Amendment right to rely on because no matter what he said that testimony couldn't be used against him. Just the other charter boat captains. This, of course, was nofuckingway land for Captain Mitch and is the point where we had first started. The chances of Captain Mitch giving up the other captains were slim to none and, as the saying goes, Slim just left town. So, for Captain Mitch, even in the impressive presence of the Hon. Howard G.

Munson, it was steady as she goes. Captain Mitch is keeping his arms folded and his powder dry and he's standing there respectfully but he's not sayin' nothin'.

A word about the Hon. Howard G. Munson. There are some people in every profession who are legendary in reputation but quite ordinary, or even less so, once you actually meet and deal with them. This would not be the case with the Hon. Howard G. Munson. Munson was the real deal. An imposing man with a booming voice and a keen intelligence to go with a sharp and rollicking sense of humor, he was virtually worshiped by the defense bar. He had tried hundreds of cases as both a trial lawyer and a judge and in a courtroom nothing escaped his attention.

Lots of lawyers and judges have war stories; but Munson had War Stories and, having landed on D-Day+6 and been wounded in the Battle of the Bulge, he was a devoted patriot and inveterate storyteller, especially if the stories were about The Big One. On the other hand, he once confided in me while leaning against a jukebox at his favorite bar with a smoldering Lucky in one hand and a Manhattan in the other that the reason he loved his job was that "Every morning I wake up knowing I can tell the Government where they get off."

Judge Munson was somewhat understanding of Captain Mitch's predicament even though he had no idea what the full back story was. But the law was the law, a Grand Jury subpoena was serious business, and if the Government wanted Munson to extend use immunity to Captain Mitch to compel his testimony, then that was how it was gonna go. Forcefully, but without any rancor, Munson told Mitch that if he failed to testify as ordered, the Judge would have no choice but to immediately put Captain Mitch in jail until either he changed his mind or the Grand Jury's term expired. Most Federal Grand Juries sit for 18 months. Some sit longer.

So now that Captain Mitch had gotten the message, Craig marched him back up to the 8th floor and the Grand Jury room, fully confident that he was going to have Captain Mitch name names and that finally the Great Little Galloo Shootout Case was now going to get solved.

No fucking way. Captain Mitch's reappearance before the Grand Jury this time was shorter than the first one and back we go to Judge Munson's courtroom.

Now, you might have noticed that throughout this saga I had not done or accomplished a heck of a lot and by and large I was acting like the proverbial potted plant. I couldn't have gone into the Grand Jury room with Captain Mitch and I certainly wasn't going to turn into an advocate for the Government and try and persuade him to change his mind. That wasn't my place even if I had an inclination to do so. But now that we were at DefCon One, I had to do something, especially when the first words from Munson's mouth were, "Mr. Menkin, has your client brought his toothbrush?"

By now at was about 4:00 p.m. on a Friday afternoon. I couldn't argue for bail because bail in a case like this is not available. I asked to approach the bench. I am not embarrassed to confess that I tried then and there to capitalize on the goodwill I had accumulated with Judge Munson over the many years I had appeared in his Court. It wasn't much of a secret that I was one of his favorites. Craig knew it; I certainly knew it.

So I employed the age-old strategy inevitably born of

Death on the Doorstep

desperation: say please. "Judge, look, the guy is obviously stubborn. Give me some more time to try and convince him there might be other options [I had no idea what these could be]. It's Friday afternoon. It's after 4:00 o'clock. The Grand Jurors probably want to go home for the weekend. I want to go home for the weekend. Give me until Monday. Nothing's gonna change between now and then."

Whether Judge Munson's affection for me played a role I know not. My guess is that he was thinking of the Grand Jurors upstairs who probably and deservedly wanted to go home that Friday afternoon. In any case, the gods of benevolence had descended and I was able to walk out of the Federal Building that afternoon with Captain Mitch in tow and not in cuffs, satisfied that at least I had done something for him and gotten a brief reprieve. We were both tired so we agreed he would call me the next day.

Not with a Bang, but with a Whimper

You practice law long enough and you learn that the perfect resolution of every case is the one where everybody goes away unhappy. Captain Mitch's adventure into criminal law had the perfect resolution.

After his somewhat exhausting afternoon in the Federal building, Captain Mitch found his way home back to Henderson Harbor. Word of the Grand Jury subpoena and Mitch's trips between the eighth and third floors and then back again had already preceded him at dockside and the captains were waiting for him. Once again, I wasn't privy to the drama, but it didn't take long for them to decide on a course of action. And, being men of action, it didn't take long to execute their plan. They would all step up, at once, and as one. They weren't going to let the Government keep squeezing Mitch who they all knew well before that weekend as the original standup guy.

So, the following Monday, I didn't have to bring Captain Mitch or his toothbrush back into the Federal building. I just picked up the phone, called Craig, and told him that the mystery had been solved and that these North Country bandidos would be turning themselves in en masse.

Which they did. If there is an amusing part to this chapter in the story it's that it all basically happened without lawyers. The captains decided on their own how it was gonna go and it went that way. The only things the lawyers (including me) did were to appear in court at the appointed times, perform the necessary yadda, yadda, yaddas and help their clients plead guilty to federal misdemeanors. They all paid a fine, had to make a contribution to the World Wildlife Fund or the Audubon Society, and got some sort of don't-do-that-no-more probation.

It wasn't all darkness. The following Spring the DEC sent a crew over to Little Galloo with gallons of baby oil and they coated every cormorant egg they could find.

SOB STORY

I f you have a smattering of legal knowledge, or maybe you want to punish yourself by practicing criminal law, you might want a basic refresher course in Grand Juries and Indictments. Here's the starter kit: the Grand Jury is an ancient and venerable institution which arose from the Magna Carta and was intended to be a protection of the populace from any whimsical persecution the Crown might feel like indulging in on any particular day for some, any, or no reason at all. The idea was that 23 citizens were supposed to get together in secret and preliminarily screen the prosecutor's barebones case to make sure there was a reasonable basis to charge another citizen with a crime.

Over the last 500 years or so, it hasn't changed much except for the part where the Government is supposed to have an actual reason to bring charges. Upon taking their oaths of service, modern Grand Jurors are secretly fitted with dog collars and nose rings to keep their minds generally uncluttered and focused on the one thing that really matters: the degree to which the Government wants to put the hammer down on someone. You may have occasionally heard the term "runaway Grand Jury"; this is to connote the appropriate designation for a bunch of people who astonishingly don't defer to the District Attorney. These people are thereafter branded renegades and are not invited back for a second sitting.

The common wisdom shared by those who do know how Grand Juries actually work was famously described by the former Chief Judge of the New York Court of Appeals, Sol Wachtler: "a grand jury would indict a ham sandwich, if that's what the D.A. wanted." Wachtler, a brilliant and very charming guy, got to be famous for other and far more interesting reasons, mostly a randy inclination to stalk a former mistress in a way ill-befitting a Judge of the New York Court of Appeals, or, in fact, even a decent human being, but that's neither here nor there for now. He went to federal prison, but he was right on about Grand Juries.

Grand Juries sit in secret, usually in small auditoria where they listen to the witnesses the DA decides to parade in. On rare occasions, they'll listen to the person whose fate is in their hands – the "target" of their inquiry – but that's pretty infrequent and is almost guaranteed to do no good. In my 40 plus years on the front lines, I've almost always advised my clients to avoid appearing before Grand Juries, mainly on the not so unreasonable assumption that once you've dropped your knickers for the prosecutor who gets to ask you pretty much anything at all (including how you cheated on your high school chemistry midterm), it's a tad difficult to put your underpants back on and go to trial to sing the same song the Grand Jury decided they didn't very much like at all.

I did have one client who insisted on going into the Grand Jury to tell his side of what happened. He was an African American guy named Big Joe who had been charged with manslaughter. He was a very nice guy; he also happened to be enormous and weighed well over 350 pounds, and not someone I'd generally be inclined to argue with.

Big Joe had had a late-night hankering for some Chinese food and pulled into the crowded parking lot of The Number One Kitchen. The Number One Kitchen was an excellent place to pick up pork lo mein, a few egg rolls, and an eightball after midnight, and the darkened parking lot was filled with the denizens of the night, very few of whom were interested in Szechuan cuisine. Joe's about to get out of his car when this puny twit in a hoodie –whose name was Taiquan something but everyone called him Hoodie – staggers up to Big Joe's car window and starts selling him a wolf ticket over a recent grievance – a girl, a debt, the weather, an imagined whatever – through a drug-hazed anger that was hard to miss. Hoodie's grievance rant is catching some vague interest from those citizens who are milling about in search of their own special high for the evening, but nobody's really paying much serious attention to any of this since Hoodie is a nasty but smallish junkie and everyone else knows that 350 pound Big Joe can handle this.

All that changes at warp speed when Hoodie pulls out a 9mm and sticks it through the window and into Joe's face. This has now gotten everyone's attention, most especially Big Joe's. With a hand the size of a catcher's mitt, Joe grabs the gun and bends Hoodie's wrist back. Painfully back. Hoodie cries out and, according to Joe, then shoots himself full in the face and falls to the pavement in a crumpled heap. Deciding that he's suddenly lost his appetite for moo shoo pork, Big Joe hits the gas and drives off into the night, not being terribly inclined to gather notarized witness statements or wait around for the police to show up.

Which they do. It would ordinarily be just another night at the South Side office for these coppers, but viewing the crumpled remains of Citizen Hoodie on the tarvia brings barely suppressed happiness to these soldiers of the State. To them, Hoodie has been a whole lot more than simply a pain in the ass low level drug dealer; he'd accumulated twelve or so felony arrests, did time for rape and child sexual abuse, and they liked him big time for two open robberies. None of the witnesses in the parking lot were grieving much for the loss of Hoodie either, and were reluctant to give up Big Joe, a well-liked guy.

Still and all, parking lot security cameras being what they were (even The Number One Kitchen owner installed one after a heart to heart from the zone commander convinced him that drug dealing in his parking lot was not just bad for the neighborhood but would be very bad, in fact terminally bad, for his business), it didn't take long for the police to track down Big Joe and invite him down to CID for a chat. Which they did.

The cops were divided into two camps: one group wanted to just clear a homicide and charge Joe with something less than murder; the other group wanted to drive him to City Hall for Citizen of the Year honors. The first group won out, not because they were outnumbered (they weren't, by a large margin) but because one of their number was the zone commander. So they charged Joe with manslaughter and he spent a night in the clink, got released on easy bail, and came to see me. He told me the story as best he remembered it and without any bravado. Having performed the minor miracle of being an African American male in the hood who made it into his early 30's without ever having been arrested or even stopped by the cops counted for something for sure; if anything, it increased his fear that something bad was going to happen to him now.

I explained what was ahead and I went through the coming steps and stages, indictment, motions, maybe plea bargaining, a trial. I told him that the case was going to be presented to a Grand Jury which would probably return an Indictment and I told him that he had a right to testify in front of the Grand Jury if he wanted to but in my opinion this was a very bad idea. For one thing, you don't get immunity and your testimony can be used against you. For another, even though as his lawyer I was entitled to be in the room with him, I couldn't ask any questions or make any objections to what the DA or the jurors would do or say. And there's no judge in there to keep order.

This part of my standard client conversation usually lasts 20 or 30 seconds at most and we move on. Not this time. Big Joe seemed interested and couldn't understand why 23 people wouldn't see it his way that Hoodie actually shot himself; at worst, even if they thought he did shoot Hoodie, it was in self-defense. And as I said earlier, Big Joe had the sort of presence you'd ordinarily not be inclined to argue with (except for the recently departed and not so lamented Hoodie who didn't get that memo), so we spent some more time talking about it. We wind up going in. Because Big Joe felt the need to tell his story.

The case was assigned to ADA Nick DeMartino, a genuinely good and upright guy who if he didn't grow up to be a lawyer would have been a priest. And that's a compliment. Nicky had smarts and compassion but, like all good lawyers, he also liked very much to win. Nicky's compassion had its limits though and it didn't extend too far past somebody getting shot in the face in a crowded parking lot at night. Even if that someone was demonstrably a low life who was a frequent flyer in the express lane to state prison.

So, at the appointed hour, Big Joe and I join Nicky in the Grand Jury room and the very first thing I pick up on is an audible gasp from some of the jurors. As I walk by one of the front desks, I hear one juror whisper, "Jesus, look at the size of this fuckin' guy." Not an auspicious start.

Joe tells his story. We rehearsed it pretty well and there wasn't a whole lot to tell anyway, so it takes, tops, three minutes. He tells it pretty well and I'm thinking, so far so good. And then. And then….Joe does something completely unrehearsed, unthought of, and just plain brilliant. He starts crying. A lot. Now, I can't answer for you, but the sight of a truly fat and large man blubbering like a six-year-old makes me feel pretty helpless myself. The Grand Jury secretary brings Big Joe a box of tissues. He blows his nose and apologizes. Nicky was at a loss as to what to do. I certainly wasn't gonna do anything. Nicky asks a few perfunctory questions and we leave.

Since Grand Jury deliberations are secret, I have no idea what Nicky told them about self-defense or self-pity or whatever they discussed but I'll bet my kids' bar mitzvah money the only thing the jurors thought about and remembered was Big Joe crying.

They gave him a pass and didn't indict him for anything. I'd love to proudly tell you this was the product of my brilliant and exceptional lawyer skills. Not. I will tell you this: I was smart enough not to test the Fates for the rest of my career and never again took the chance of putting a client into the Grand Jury. If there's crying to be done, they can leave it to me.

STAN COLLELLA'S WHITE CONVERTIBLE

Things were getting grimmer by the day in the cavernous Federal courtroom of the Hon. Howard G. Munson. My assigned client, Jack Zogby, was charged along with four other guys with racketeering, not your garden variety kind of crime. We were two weeks into the trial and the jury was being served a prosecutorial smorgasbord of murder, bombing, extortion, and moving stolen property. And it wasn't helping things much that my client's nickname was "Turk"; even though he was Syrian, everyone called him Turk, even his wife. And here's a practice tip: if you've got to go to trial in a racketeering case, try to avoid having your client referred to as "Turk" in the Indictment. Not a great optic.

The charges were bad enough, but The Turk had brought along his own colorful history to the case, something which particularly energized the prosecutors. Turk was 66 years old and was working on his seventh felony conviction. That would be seventh. One of the major demerits on his report card had occurred some fifteen years earlier when he was part of the Mob hit team that took down Al Marrone, a ferocious player in his own right, on an Albany street one night. (When the admitting ER nurse asked Marrone's girlfriend what his occupation was, she said "gangster." It's part of the hospital record to this day.)

Despite some of his apparent shortcomings, though, The Turk was a good client, cooperative, and appreciative. Regrettably, his case, along with that of his four codefendants, wasn't going so good that day, or any other day since the first day of trial. It wasn't much more than a painfully slow guilty plea.

Tommy Bretti was on the stand explaining to the jury how the bomb that Michael Andrello had fashioned out of a tackle box and filled with nails and screws had gone off on his porch as he had approached his front yard, grievously injuring him. It exploded because Jack Minicone had set it off from across the street using a remote-control servo that Andrello had given him. And the reason Minicone was across the street with the servo was because his initial effort the day before came to naught when Bretti drove off from the parking lot of Grimaldi's Ristorante where Minicone had originally placed the bomb under Bretti's car and Andrello's bomb didn't go off because the first servo didn't work. Minicone wound up having words with Andrello for his shoddy workmanship. But now Minicone was twenty feet from us at one of the defense tables and only ten feet from Bretti with whom he was having a staring contest.

It was grim and dramatic testimony. The jury was riveted. For Turk and me? not so much. For one thing, we had heard this story maybe a dozen times in the past. For another, and far more importantly, the event had nothing at all to do with The Turk, and in fact he and Bretti happened to be friends. Leaving the stand later and slowly walking out of the courtroom, Bretti made it a point to glare at Minicone as he walked past the defense tables, but when he got to Turk he leaned over and gave him a high-five, saying, loud enough for the jury to hear "How you doin' babe?"

The tension of the morning had had its expected effect on everyone and by 12:15 we were all drained and it was time for lunch. Since Turk, Minicone, and Tony Inserra had each been denied bail, they had to go down in the blocks for the noon hour. It was a beautiful Spring and I always felt badly that Turk was denied the opportunity to dine al fresco at lunchtime. But the families for the incarcerated guys made up for it by bringing in trays of mannicot, lasagna, and eggplant parm to dine on. The guards shared in it too.

I escaped the Federal building in the company of two of my co-counsel, the always elegant Emil Rossi and the always fun Joe Fahey. We walked out to glorious sunshine and an azure blue sky. As we approached the corner, we came upon a brand spanking new white Toyota convertible stopped at the light with Stan Colella sitting behind the wheel.

A word about Stan. He was a short, somewhat chubby, handsome Italian, a musician, a truly lovely guy who was well known in the community especially for his work with teen musicians. He had his own band, playing gigs like bar mitzvahs and weddings, but in the summers he used to organize a teen orchestra which toured around parks and various community events. Everyone knew Stan, everyone liked him. And of course, since he was a Colella and Emil was a Colella and they were cousins on Emil's mother's side, they start in on a conversation, particularly about Stan's brand-new car.

Joe and I are just standing there, anxious to get to lunch. Probably because I have this compulsion to be funny whenever I can, I turn to Joe and, gesturing to Stan's car, I say "Hey, Joe. The Turk told me that if I walk him, he's gonna get me one of these." Joe laughs. I laugh. Emil & Stan are done chatting. We go to lunch.

The trial resumed and the afternoon's testimony wasn't anywhere near as interesting as Tommy Bretti's. In fact, it really had nothing to do with Turk at all, so he and I passed the time at our table in quiet idle conversation. Because I thought that he might be amused at my clever remark to Joe about Stan Colella's car, I tell him the story of the street-side conversation. When I get to "Hey, Joe. The Turk told me that if I walk him, he's gonna get me one of these," The Turk looks at me with his dark Syrian eyes and says, thoughtfully and seriously, "Yeah? where does this guy live?"

I crack up. Had we not been in the middle of a huge courtroom and engaged in a deadly serious trial, I would have fallen off my chair.

I probably told that story two dozen times after the trial. (Turk and everybody else got convicted, sadly a foregone conclusion).

So now it's six months later. I'm down at the Y and I go into the steam room next to the men's locker. There are three guys sitting there, all balls naked and luxuriating in the sweetly stinging humidity. I take my place on the bench and just minutes later, joining our little schvitzing fraternity, in comes Stan Colella. I greet him, "Hey, Stan! How you doing?" and he responds with "Hey, Eddie! Good to see ya." Stan finds room on the bench opposite me, between two naked guys.

Never one to pass up a situation to tell what I think is a funny story, even in a room where everyone is stark naked, I start telling Stan the story of Turk's comment about Stan's car. I'm in a tiled room. I have a loud voice, I know this. The three other naked guys are hanging on every word. I get to the punchline, "Yeah? where does this guy live?" and the three naked guys roar. I look at Stan. He's white as a sheet.

I tell him, "Stan, don't worry about it. Turk got seven years. By the time he's out, you'll have a different car." Stan still didn't think it was funny.

Memo to self: never tell someone a story that you think is funny unless you are pretty sure they will think it's funny too.

A JURY'S WISDOM

Juries don't always get it right. But jurors always really want to do the right thing.

I once represented a young guy named Mike. He was about 20 and he lived with his parents in a nice neat suburban house. He had an older sister named Susan. Susan was a teacher and a very responsible type.

So one summer weekend Mike's parents are away and it's an open house for Mike and about 50 of his closest friends. Susan gets wind of it, so she comes over to chaperone and to try and keep the damage to an acceptable level.

Things get noisy and on the verge of out of hand, so the local police come over to thin out the crowd and things quiet down. And the police leave. No harm, no foul.

The beer starts to run out around midnight and people start leaving. So now it's about 2:00 o'clock in the morning and Mike is sitting on a rocking chair on the front porch and the only people left in the house are Susan who is now upstairs sleeping and Mike's friend Freddy who is sitting at the kitchen table finishing off the 12 pack of Bud light that he brought over.

Two cop cars come rolling up on the front lawn and the police approach the front door. It's an open screen door and straight through they can see Freddy nursing his 12 pack. The cops ignore Mike and open the door and start walking towards Freddy at the kitchen table. Mike gets up from the rocker and follows the cops, asking what they want and why are they in the house. They ignore him. This doesn't sit well with Mike and he yells "This is bullshit!" They still ignore him.

Their interest is in Freddy who, unbeknownst to Mike, had made a beer run down to the nearby 7-11 and somehow forgot to pay for the 12 pack he had hoisted on his shoulder when he left. So now voices are raised and Susan, who had been sleeping upstairs, comes down in her pajamas and wants to know what's going on. Getting no answer, and being annoyed at the whole thing, she blurts out "This is bullshit!" Mike starts to get really agitated and he starts moving towards the cops. Susan sees it, moves towards Mike, slips on beer that's all over the floor and bumps into one of the cops.

The cops then leave, but not before handcuffing Freddy, handcuffing Susan, and telling Mike he better calm down because they're tired of hearing "This is bullshit." Now it's about 2:30 in the morning and Mike is so beside himself that he follows the police car with Susan in the back all the way to the police station where he complains to the desk sergeant that, "All of this is just bullshit!" Mike then gets arrested and the three of them spend the night in the clink.

I try and settle the case with the DA, who doesn't look kindly on noisy suburban beer parties and even though the police didn't have a warrant to enter the house looking for Freddy and his stolen beer, he wants Mike and Susan to plead guilty to Disorderly Conduct and write letters of apology to the police. I probably don't have to tell you what they said in response to the settlement offer.

So we have an honest to goodness trial in Town Court and a jury of 6 hardworking citizens have to sit through a parade of police officers recounting the saga of their search and apprehension of Freddy cold-handed with his 12-pack in Mike's kitchen and how rude Mike and Susan were to them. It takes all day. My summation is as low-key as I can manage under the circumstances, but the essence of the summation is "Folks, this is bullshit."

The Judge gives the jury their final instructions and they file out to deliberate. I badly need a cigarette, so I walk out the side door with the nice young DA who tried the case. I tell him, "Look, this really is bullshit. It's still not too late. You can still dismiss this." He starts telling me that he'll go easy when it comes down to sentencing. The Court Clerk comes out to tell us the Jury is back. It hasn't been three minutes since they went in to deliberate. I say, "Do they want an exhibit?" She says, "No, they have a verdict."

So we go back in and hear "Not Guilty." Not the greatest verdict I ever took, but naturally I was happy for Mike and Susan and their family.

I'm getting my papers together and the foreman of the jury comes over to me and says I did a very good job. Always nice to hear, and I thank him. I then ask him, how come it only took three minutes? He says "We all walked into the room and nobody sat down. I turned to the other 5 and said, 'This is bullshit' and we all agreed."

Well, it was. It was bullshit. Jurors always want to do the right thing.

THUNDER FROM HOWIE THE HORSE

No one delivered judicial thunder like Howie the Horse. He was a big man with a face fit for Mount Rushmore and an endless supply of war stories. And not just lawyer war stories, although he had plenty of those too. He proudly served in the Big One, was wounded at the Battle of the Bulge, and knew more about Von Rundstedt's Ardennes campaign than most lawyers know about torts. Lawyers loved trying cases before him not only because he had tried hundreds of cases as a trial lawyer before becoming a Federal District Court Judge with lifetime tenure but also because he was smart, tolerant, and funny. He once told me that he loved his job because "I wake up every morning knowing that I get to tell the Government every day where they get off." My hero.

Yeah, he was funny, very funny. He was pretty compassionate when it came to sentencing too. But he was no one to mess with and he had his limits. His volcanic eruptions were slow in coming but when the acid and the ash finally started blowing no one escaped. And if the incineration of the first blast didn't do the job, the full sonic boom of his basso profundo shook what remained of your skeleton. He was otherwise, even for a judge, a fun guy to appear in front of. You just didn't want to get crosswise with him.

A bunch of us were doing our best to fend off the Government's proof and witnesses (which were coming in volleys like fireballs) but the magnitude of the case and the depth of our clients' guilt (there were five of us) made getting through this trial not much different than swimming against a cold ocean tide after a shipwreck. Howie the Horse recognized this and although not sympathetic to any of us, at least gave us room to breathe if we tried to put in a defense. One of our number, Bobby G., had been testing Howie's limits and patience all trial, stumbling over pointless questions and making objections based on legal theories known only to himself. Given the stakes of this RICO case, where gangland bombings and hits were just part of an overlong movie script, Bobby G. was pressing any luck he may have ever accumulated in his lifetime.

Bobby G. was a lawyer who had a last name but hardly anybody knew it. This was mainly and probably because it was too hard to pronounce. Or spell. Court stenographers were hopelessly lost somewhere between the Cyrillic alphabet and their Armenian thesaurus and most judges simply went along with everybody from the coffee shop busboy to Mrs. Delvecchio, the super-efficient clerk of the court, and just referred to him as Mr. Bobby G. Even Howie the Horse, who had enough natural radar to spare and then put some on loan to NASA referred to him as "Mr. G."

Of course, jurors and those similarly disinterested in what was going on in the courtroom probably all thought that the guy's name was actually Gi or Gia or Gee and otherwise paid this no mind. That may also have had something to do with the fact that when Bobby G. spoke he rarely had anything of interest or intelligence to say. To anybody. This naturally was a recurring disappointment to those of his clients who understood English in the first place and this, too, was a pretty elite group. Their main and native language always seemed to be cash, a lingua franca which Bobby G. spoke fluently and understood quite well.

This time, however, what Bobby G. had just said was definitely of interest to Howie the Horse.

Bobby was summing up (brilliantly, in his opinion) and he had just said something along the lines of "If Freddie Mustico was so darn important to the Government's case, how come they didn't call him as a witness and you didn't hear from him?"

Excuse me?

Those of us who had been even vaguely listening had pretty much the same question as Howie. How could anybody with a shred of common sense, not to mention common decency, bring up Freddie Mustico?

Cutting off this Bobby G. peroration and unleashing a sudden blast of judicial thunder (while still restraining himself mightily), Howie boomed "I'll see counsel in chambers."

To those of us who had previously waged battle in assorted criminal wars before Howie the Horse, this was, we knew, not just an early storm warning. This was more in the mode of the sudden computerized reverse 911 phone call informing you that a flaming three mile wide meteor was hurtling towards your house and you had, say, two, three minutes tops to clear out because your neighborhood, if not the entire planet, was about to be destroyed. This was not good. Sphincters tightened and stomachs roiled. We all knew some frightening event was about to unfold.

The back story of Freddie Mustico was a pretty grim one. So grim, in fact, that it had haunted Howie the Horse for the duration of his long judicial career. In their efforts to indict Ernie Mouzzone, the Feds had served a Grand Jury subpoena on Mustico on the not so illogical theory that his business as a major bookie had attracted Mouzzone's interest and, as practically everybody knew, Mouzzone had been extorting protection money from Mustico for years.

To say that Mustico was reluctant to testify against Mouzzone was an understatement. In fact, Mustico was not only scared shitless of Mouzzone (joining a fairly large group of the shitless in the Utica area), but his lawyer was equally terrified. So the lawyer goes to Howie and asks him to quash the subpoena. Recognizing that being scared shitless is not among the very limited grounds to quashing a Grand Jury subpoena, Howie explains to the lawyer that Mustico has two and only two unattractive choices: testify or sit in jail until he's ready to testify. The lawyer is ashen and sweating profusely, not sure what is worse: having Mustico testify or telling Mustico he has to testify. Howie remains firm and the lawyer departs. Mustico testifies in front of the Grand Jury.

A week later, a guy carrying a shotgun and wearing a ski mask walks into a barbershop and blows Freddie Mustico away. In front of his young child. The gunman goes unidentified but generally fits the size and shape of Ernie Mouzzone. Mustico had had his own cast of sketchy competitors and people who owed him money and they too could have wielded that shotgun. But most people in the know believed it was Mouzzone, someone who had benefitted bigly from the periodic past disappearances or unexplained absences of people who had somehow gotten crosswise with him.

The Feds, of course, were beside themselves with outrage and argued forcefully in support of getting proof of Mustico's demise into Mouzzone's trial. But, as guilt-ridden and remorseful as he was over compelling Mustico's GJ testimony (because under the law he had to), Howie wouldn't allow the Government to introduce evidence about this awful episode. Not a provable connection to Mouzzone. Too prejudicial.

Enter Bobby G. and his special ability to step all over himself.

So, when Bobby G. started blathering in summation about where's Freddie Mustico and why didn't the Government call him as a witness, he didn't just cross the line against the rules of appropriate trial summation. He entered Howie's Valley of Death. In retrospect, "I'll see counsel in chambers" was an unbelievably restrained interruption by Howie the Horse who wasn't just outraged. He was momentarily beside himself.

The only small degree of relief we all felt was that we knew it wasn't us, it was Mr. Bobby G. who was about to be dipped into Howie's deep fryer. Sadly, however, this near universal sense of dread was not shared by Mr. G. whose only response to the gathering herd of lawyers trundling onto the ramp of the abattoir waiting in Howie's chambers was, "Why'd the Judge cut me off? I was on a freakin' roll. This is bullshit."

When the seven of us were admitted into Howie's chambers, he was standing, still in his robes and at his usual station, a well-worn brown leather sofa with a small nubby afghan carelessly crumpled on one side and the sports section of the newspaper covering scattered and assorted motions and briefing papers submitted for Howie's eventual attention in the other.

When we were lucky enough to be invited into this room at all, Howie was usually reclining on the sofa to rest his recurrently aching back (Howie said that the briefs and pleadings made an excellent lumbar support when rolled correctly) and he would be dragging deeply on a Lucky Strike. He was, of course, smoking when we walked in, but most of us knew the smoke had less to do with his Lucky and a whole lot more to do with his roiling rage at what had just happened out there. He didn't sit down, and he didn't invite us to sit either.

"Would you mind telling me what the fuck you are doing out there?" This was as gentle an opening as the Horse in his fury could manage. His deep, deep voice, seasoned with a regimen of Manhattans and Luckies over fifty or so years, would ordinarily have been perfect for the late-night mellowness of a jazz DJ on FM radio. This time, it was simply frightening.

Tom Flannerty, who had been doing the crossword puzzle during Bobby G.'s summation, knew that he probably shouldn't have had it actually out on the counsel table, but he also knew that the Horse wasn't talking to him so it was easy for Tommy to maintain a puzzled look. Bob Newman had been deep in conversation with his client, Ernie Mouzzone, during Bobby G.'s summation, talking about Juror #11, the one with the big tits that Ernie had been fixated on for the past seven weeks, but Bob didn't think that Howie either knew or cared.

Everybody looked at Bobby G. who had, in the preceding milliseconds, figured out that Howie was talking to him and that the subject must have been the last thing he was saying to the jury, to wit: the absence of testimony from the late Freddie Mustico.

"Judge," Bobby G. began, "it's fair comment. They didn't call Mustico."

"Well, of course they didn't call him, you stupid asshole!" Howie roared in full stentorian blast at Bobby G. "You know goddamned well why they didn't call him! He's dead! You know it, I know it, and your weasel client knows it. Somebody wearing a ski mask and looking just like your own fucking client blew him away in a barbershop in front of his own goddamned kid. And that happened right after I made him testify in front the Grand Jury. Is that news to you for Chrissakes?"

Howie whirled around as if to stalk off but then realized he was in his own chambers. He turned again, squinted his baggy eyes, and lifted the smoldering Lucky, quickly sweeping it at the clutch of lawyers before him. "I'll tell you all this, the next lawyer who brings up Mustico, I will personally cut his balls off and get disbarred! Now all of you get the fuck out of here!"

Relieved that it was over, at least for the moment, and that the rest of us were safe, we all started to turn away. Unbelievably, Bobby G. didn't move. Setting a new combined world record for density and recklessness, he asked, "Well, what are you gonna tell the jury, Judge?"

Howie the Horse briefly stared and said nothing, as if composing himself and his thoughts after hearing a particularly good legal point he hadn't thought of before. He lowered his voice and spoke. A slow and even distant rumble. "Well, I was considering telling them that you are perhaps the most incompetent lawyer who's ever practiced before me but that they should forgive you because you are too fucking stupid to know it. Now get out!"

This time, we all left.

It took a while for Howie to resume the bench that day.

THE ROOFTOP BURGLAR AND
A LESSON ON HEARSAY

Pretty early in my life of combat in Federal Court, I was assigned a Hobbs Act case. If you don't know what the Hobbs Act is, don't hurt your head about it because at the time I didn't either. But this particular case gave a new meaning to "learning the hard way." And though I can now look back on the whole experience with a degree of fondness and humor, at the time it was a painful uphill slog.

My client was an ex-cop who got to be an ex-cop by developing his career as a criminal while supposedly on duty. He was curiously proud of the reputation he nurtured as "The Rooftop Burglar," a nom de guerre which the local paper bestowed on him before he was caught.

The Rooftop Burglar was a guy who rather artfully broke into a whole bunch of local small businesses through skylights, vents, chimneys, and any other available apertures on the roofs of buildings, and for a long time the police couldn't catch him. A major impediment to solving this series of crimes was not, as you might expect, investigative incompetence (it was, after all, a pretty small force in a pretty small town). It had more to do with the fact that the Chief of Police assigned his crack patrolman, my client, to head up the investigation and since my guy was not particularly inclined to arrest himself the search for The Rooftop Burglar took a little longer than expected.

Getting to know him in the uniquely intimate way that only a defense lawyer gets to know his criminal client, there is no doubt in my mind that whatever objets d'art and other meaningless detritus he picked up on his rooftop forays were, for him, really beside the point. He just liked getting over on people. Especially those who employed him or gave him orders, but also people in general.

I'm not exactly sure how he got caught, but I do remember that he took an inordinate pleasure in everybody else finding out that it was him. Besides being a thief, he fancied himself a major tough guy (which, in fact he was; more about that later) and I remember him telling me that the two years he did in prison for "the RTB caper" (as he liked to call it) was something he could have done "standin' on my head." I really can't tell you how many times I have heard that particularly tired and shallow bravado from a client; my guy was about thirty two at the time he said this, but I can assure you it gets your attention when you hear it from a sixteen year old kid.

Anyhow, the RTB caper was big news in a small town and my client did his 2 years (whether it was standing on his head or not I am not sure) and he returned to his local town with major street cred (or as major as his "cred" was going to get in a burg with a twice weekly paper and an all-volunteer fire department). Having spent most of his time "inside" reading Guns and Ammo and working out in the weight room, his compact frame came out fairly well buffed and his knowledge of weaponry was pretty extensive, particularly for those types of weapons he'd never see, own, or use. Of course his conversations were enriched by his casual dropping of the names of manufacturers of several types of speed loaders, and this deeply impressed the goobers who lazed about the local bar, hung on his every word, and thought this guy was a North Country version of Tony Soprano.

None of this would have, should have, even might have gotten the attention of the Federales. In the Federal sea of criminality Mr. RTB was the equivalent of krill, a microorganism which only gets a whale's attention when it congregates with say two, three hundred thousand of its brother krill in one floating swarm. Mr. RTB didn't get the Feds' attention through his petty crimes or barroom braggadocio. He got their attention because he threatened a bank. Sort of.

Now, about the Hobbs Act. This particular federal law was passed in 1946 and it forbids extortion, particularly extortion of a bank. I'm not so sure that if the same bill came before Congress today there'd be a whole lot of support for protecting banks from anything, much less from people who are legitimately pissed at how banks get over on the rest of us. The way most people see it today, it's banks who have been extorting the rest of us. And this episode with Mr. RTB was around 1982, a time when banks were still seen as important and dignified institutions.

So one pleasant North Country Spring evening, Mr. RTB, whose name by the way was Paige, is sitting in Bobby Fleming's kitchen regaling young Bobby (he's around 23 at the time) and his homies Mike Marquette (a genuinely ferocious and terrifying guy who years later went on to kill his very pretty wife in a fit of domestic rage and then turn the shotgun on himself) and Huey Highsmith (a meth addict of singularly unattractive appearance and disposition) with tales of the Legend of The RTB and other assorted stories with no particular point other than they were about him.

The phone rings. There's sobbing at the other end. Bobby's sweet silver-haired mother is reporting that Billy Pfaff had come over around 9:00 o'clock with two of his tow trucks and repossessed both of Mr. & Mrs. Fleming's cars. They were way behind on paying Seaway National Bank for one car, but the other they owned free and clear.

This shocking injustice could not be ignored and the Legend of the RTB compelled Paige to immediately take arms against the sea of the Flemings' troubles. They all knew Billy Pfaff, a hard-working mechanic with a small garage who picked up the odd dollar here and there by repossessing cars for the local banks. Not terribly complex work: hook it up and drive off. If he met with resistance, rare as that was, he had an engaging manner and explained to the unhappy owner he'd have to take it up with the Bank. To Paige, Pfaff was a wimp. That, of course, was because everybody but him (and possibly Marquette) was a wimp.

Paige told Bobby to tell his mother that he and Marquette were going to take care of it and get the cars back. That night. They tried to recruit Huey to go with them, but he had a meetup with his dealer later on and priorities were priorities. They told Bobby to stay home because this kind of man's work was for the rough and ready and things could get ugly.

Ugly things became. They found Billy Pfaff at a local bar around 11:00 o'clock and Paige sidled up to him, turning on whatever charm he might have stored away in some forgotten place. The charm, of course, was adroitly applied along with the looming presence of Marquette at Paige's elbow. Marquette didn't say anything at all. He didn't have to, but he did keep venomously staring Pfaff full in the face and his bulk and deep scowl made it clear he was open for business.

At first, Paige says "Hey Billy, you really shouldn't have taken Mrs. Fleming's Plymouth. She don't owe the bank nuthin' on that." Pfaff says that those were his instructions; two cars, the Plymouth and the Honda. Now Paige is telling him he's got to give up both cars and Pfaff is becoming less sure about what he was told to do in the first place: "Ah, I don't know here. Let me think on it."

Paige is becoming disappointed. And a little agitated. He then levels his stare at Billy Pfaff and says in a low and menacing voice, "I tell ya what Billy Boy. You know who I am. You know what my reputation is around here. You really don't need your garage and trucks firebombed. All you gotta do is tell me where the cars are. Simple as that. Easy peezy. No trouble for you. Just tell me."

Pfaff, now quaking, tells Paige he's gotta make some calls and Paige watches Pfaff go over to a phone booth. It takes maybe a half an hour, but Pfaff comes back to Paige, tells him where the cars can be found, and spends the rest of the night rethinking whether he really does need to stay in the repo business.

If you are thinking that Paige had committed a crime by threatening Pfaff and extorting information from him through the threat of violence, you would be correct and would earn a B+ in criminal law this semester. If, on the other hand, you recognized that by standing in a noisy Watertown bar and scaring the bejesus out of Billy Pfaff, the RTB was committing a Federal crime by threatening to extort property from a federally insured bank (remember the Hobbs act?) you can take the rest of the semester off with a well-earned A.

And that is how we wound up in a creaky old Federal courthouse some months later in Auburn, New York on trial before the notoriously unpleasant Hon. Lloyd F. MacMahon, a Federal judge who was appointed to the Federal bench by President Eisenhower and who regarded most of the twentieth century as some irritating sick novelty act. MacMahon ate attorneys for lunch and picked his teeth with the bones of lawyers he had sent to jail for contempt or simply displeasing him. He once actually told a jury that acquitted some poor guy of tax evasion that they were the stupidest bunch of people he ever met. Another time, when he ran out of prospective jurors in Manhattan, he directed the courtroom deputy marshal to go outside and get the guy selling Sabrett's hotdogs on the corner to be Juror #12. (True story.) He was also fond of throwing things, especially his robe, which on more than one occasion he bundled up in fury and tossed in a rage as he left the bench for the day. (He did it on the day he died.) He was a very smart guy, the smartest Judge around; all you had to do was ask him.

So you can imagine what a treat this trial was going to be: defending an egotistical thug on a really exotic federal criminal charge of extorting a working guy (but really the bank) in front of a judge who took "good morning, Your Honor" as a potential insult. And, to add to the outright strangeness of the whole thing, this was 1982 and the case was being prosecuted by a woman, Assistant United States Attorney Nancy Jones, something guaranteed to put MacMahon on edge, especially because Nancy was a good-looking woman.

Nancy's attractiveness created a minor dilemma for MacMahon: he liked good looking women generally, but this was, after all, 1982 and, being a misogynist of his time, a female lawyer confused him, no matter how good looking she was. (MacMahon died in 1989 but I guarantee that if he was alive today he would regard the #MeToo movement as a subversive communist conspiracy.)

The Government's case seemed fairly straightforward. Paige threatened Pfaff who was employed by a federally insured bank and he extorted property, "something of value" (i.e., information about where the repossessed cars were located). The fact that one of the cars was wrongfully repossessed counted somewhere between legally irrelevant and Judge McMahon didn't want to hear about it. Well, of course, the prosecution calls Billy Pfaff and he did a pretty good job of replicating the fear he was feeling when Paige was staring him in the face.

Nancy then gets Pfaff to tell the jury who he called after his face to face with Paige. That would be Ms. Kareta Noone, the then vice president of the bank, a lady who labored through life without either charm or a sense of humor. So Pfaff starts telling the jury what he told Kareta. So far, I guess, that's OK. Then, to no one's surprise, including mine, Nancy starts having Pfaff relate to the jury what Kareta told him. Now, even if the foundation of most of your legal knowledge is television (and, I should observe, this is also sadly true of far too many lawyers), whatever Kareta told Pfaff pretty much met the classic definition of hearsay (an out of court statement offered to prove the truth of the matter asserted).

However, I was up against two truths which were then looming large: a) we were in Federal Court and the Federal Rules of Evidence have more exceptions to the Hearsay Rule than there are Rules to begin with, and b) we were in Judge McMahon's courtroom. Still, I object and MacMahon reacts with a condescending grimace, overruling my objection with a sneer which clearly signaled his displeasure with me getting in the way of the steam engine of justice.

Despite my objection ("it's hearsay, Your Honor"), Pfaff says that he told Kareta word for word what Paige's threats were, asks her what he should do, and she tells him to stand by, hold on, she's gonna check with the President of the Bank, Carmen Palumbo. Then, Pfaff tells us, Kareta calls him back after her conversation with Palumbo and tells Pfaff what Palumbo said. At that point, I'm thinking, for Christ's sakes Judge, this is hearsay on top of hearsay, there are no exceptions to it, and this isn't right.

I object again on these grounds, leaving off the "for Christ's sakes" part. MacMahon overrules my objections telling me that I'll have my chance to question Kareta and Palumbo since they are on the Government's witness list. It was true enough that we were going to hear from Kareta and Palumbo, but that doesn't satisfy me or make me any happier because hearsay is hearsay and who knows what version these later witnesses are going to come up with?

And if Paige's words had been distorted, then there really may not have been a crime here at all. But, he's the Judge and even though it's still early in my career, I know enough not to get too crosswise with Lloyd MacMahon. At least not yet.

The upshot of Pfaff's testimony was that Kareta told him, apparently on Palumbo's instructions, to tell Paige where the

Flemings' cars could be found. And he did that. And the Flemings got their cars back that night. Temporarily.

Next up on the witness stand was Kareta Noone and she, of course, relates how she got a late-night phone call from the terrified Billy Pfaff. We already have this information. Now, however, we are into a fresh round of double and triple hearsay because she tells us, over my repeated objections, about the conversation she had with Palumbo who, apparently, called the police who told him it was late, they had other things to do that night, and that the Bank should just return the cars and everything would get sorted out in daylight. So that's apparently what Palumbo instructed Kareta to tell Pfaff. You following all of this?

At this point, I'm not quite giving up objecting but I need to get past MacMahon's dyspepsia and aversion to allow the defense to point out that that evening turned into a Chinese fire drill of multiple conversations of differing versions of what Paige actually may have said, and since we are getting hearsay upon hearsay it can't really be said that Paige was actually threatening a bank. Which, of course, was what he was charged with.

Seeing as the Judge was being less than helpful, my last resort was to try to get past him and make it clear to the jury how ridiculous this kind of "evidence" was since either Judge MacMahon wasn't getting it or he didn't really care. (Pretty sure it was "really didn't care.") My cross-examination of the utterly humorless Kareta Noone went like this:

"So, Ms. Noone, you get a phone call from Billy Pfaff in the middle of the night, is that right."

"Yes."

"And he tells you Paige has threatened him unless he tells

him where the cars are. Is that Right?"

"Yes."

"So you tell him you're going to check with Palumbo and get back to him. Is that what you did?"

"Yes."

"And then you called Carmen Palumbo and you told him that Pfaff had called you and you told him what Paige had said to Pfaff? Is that how it went?"

"Yes."

"You never spoke that night with Paige, isn't that so?

"Yes."

"So whatever Paige is supposed to have said to Pfaff, you got Pfaff's version, right?"

"Yes."

"And when you told Palumbo all of this, he told you that he was going to call the police and he would get back to you, right?"

"Yes. That's right."

"As far as you know, Palumbo never spoke to Pfaff, right?"

"No, he didn't talk to Pfaff."

"And Palumbo never spoke to Paige, right?"

"No, he never spoke to Paige."

"So Palumbo does get back to you and he tells you the police said to have Pfaff tell Paige where the cars were and it would all get straightened out the next day? Isn't that right?"

"Yes."

"So, tell me, Ms. Noone, do you know whether or not Palumbo told the police what you told him Pfaff told you Paige said to him?"

And, of course, she said "Yes." Even MacMahon got the

point.

Given what I had to work with, then, my thinking was that at that point in the trial – despite Judge MacMahon giving aid and comfort to the Government – I had done a fairly good job of creating some degree of doubt (always the defendant's friend) as to a) what had Paige actually said to Pfaff in the first place? and b) did he intend to threaten a bank? (He wasn't charged with threatening poor Billy Pfaff; the jury had to find that for all intents and purposes, Billy Pfaff was the bank.)

Nancy didn't actually think she was losing the case at this point, but she was astute enough to recognize that she needed to button up the question of Paige's intent. It should be fairly obvious to you, as you read this story, what Paige's intent was; but there's a big difference between what is mildly amusing in a trial lawyer's story and what is proof beyond a reasonable doubt in a criminal trial.

So Nancy looks around for a witness who could tell the jury in clear terms what Paige's intent was. Paige himself was unavailable, being the defendant and all and not inclined to take the stand. Ditto for young Bobby Fleming who, for reasons which remain mysterious to me to this day, wound up getting indicted even though he never took the trip over to the bar to chat with Billy Pfaff. The fearsome Mike Marquette, he of the silent menace and holding a ringside seat at the Flemings' kitchen table when the "plot" was hatched, was apparently in the wind and not available. Why Marquette was not indicted was also a mystery to me, but it is an unwritten code amongst criminal defense lawyers not to complain to the prosecutor that there should be more defendants sitting at the courtroom table. When it comes to summation to the jury, however, all bets on this subject are off and it is somewhere between common and always that defense lawyers will blame the empty chair.

So it was not a huge surprise to me that before we start business one afternoon, Nancy stands up and informs Judge MacMahon that her next witness is Mr. Huey Highsmith, full time North Country meth head. However, Nancy notes that there was a "preliminary matter" which the Court had to address. I know what's coming and I don't like it much.

What is coming is Huey, in the company of two FBI agents, slouching, scuffling, and scowling, wearing a drab green jumpsuit, leg irons and a set of handcuffs affixed uncomfortably to a chain around his waist. He's not dressed for success. A name tag pasted on his chest with "Reluctant Witness" scrawled in magic marker would not have been out of place.

Nancy announces to the Judge that Mr. Highsmith is "reluctant" to testify. He's currently incarcerated just up the street in Auburn prison working off what's left of a minor drug beef and he doesn't appreciate the day trip over to Federal Court. Nancy tells MacMahon that Huey intends to invoke his 5th Amendment right to remain silent and not be a witness against himself. The Government is requesting that the Court grant Huey immunity so that whatever he says cannot be used against him. In fact, it is lost on no one – most especially Huey – that he didn't really need immunity in the first place because sitting at Bobby Fleming's kitchen table did not amount to much, least of all a crime, and, immunity or not, he just wasn't inclined to talk to anyone about this. Not Nancy. Not the Judge. Not the Jury. Nobody.

Huey is now slouching in the witness chair, in full shackle

mode, and MacMahon, from less than five feet away, is explaining to him in a loud and irritated voice what immunity means and that if he refuses to testify he can be held in contempt of Court. Huey stares blankly back at MacMahon and says nothing. Exasperated, MacMahon then shouts at him, "Do you hear me? Do you understand what I'm telling you? Do you understand that if you don't testify here I can put you in jail?"

Huey silently raises his shackled wrists in MacMahon's direction and says, "I'm already in fuckin' jail mister."

Huey is excused.

Nobody talks to MacMahon that way. He is ballistic and beside himself with rage. So he focuses on the nearest blameworthy target of opportunity. That would be me. He glares at me and says, "I suspect witness tampering here. I've been in this business too long not to know it when I see it. I'm ordering a complete investigation into this and" at this point his wagging his finger directly at me, "whoever is responsible is going to jail for ten years." And with that, he stands up and is heading off the bench into his chambers.

Forget MacMahon, I am beside myself. I had never met Huey Highsmith in my life and really doubted that whatever this meth head was going to say would have made any difference at all in the trial. So I manage to get off, "Your Honor" but MacMahon cuts me off on his way out of the courtroom by shouting "I don't want to hear it." And he's through the side door.

I collect myself for a few minutes and decide this is USDA certified bullshit that will not stand. So I find my way through a twisting warren of small hallways behind the old courtroom to find the Judge. I run into Jim Evans, the Judge's very tall courtroom deputy clerk, and tell him that when Nancy is free I want to speak with the Judge. Jim quietly chuckles and says, "You're a brave guy Eddie."

Nancy thinks that this is all moderately amusing, so she joins me in the hallway and soon enough His Ferociousness appears at the doorway of his chambers, with Big Jim looming behind him, smiling. MacMahon says, "What do you want?" I tell him that I didn't appreciate being accused in open court of tampering with a witness. MacMahon, waves me off, "I wasn't talking about you. I was talking about your jerk of a client. You had nothing to do with it." I tell him it didn't look that way out there (and I get a nod of quiet assent from smiling Big Jim who's standing behind the Judge). MacMahon says, "Ah, forget about it," wheels around, and goes back into his chambers. I'm hardly comforted but I'm feeling that at least I stood up for myself.

We resume about twenty minutes later. As MacMahon comes out of the side door, trailed by Big Jim, he announces to the bailiff "Hold the jury." OK, I'm thinking, now what?

The Judge calls us up to the bench and with the stenographer present puts an apology to me on the record, saying he didn't mean to accuse me of anything, that I was a fine lawyer, and I have been doing an excellent job for my client. Nancy is astonished. I'm astonished. It's not as if it wasn't deserved; it's just that given MacMahon's history with lawyers it was simply unheard of.

To this day, I still credit Big Jim for talking MacMahon down off the ledge during the break and explaining to him that even for him he was out of line. (Some law clerks do have that kind of license with some judges.)

I got a transcript of MacMahon's apology and held on to it

for quite a while just in the off chance some lawyers wouldn't believe this part of the story. Most didn't. The transcript is now probably tucked away in a long-forgotten file, MacMahon died about seven years later, and Paige got all of two years in Federal prison for his tough guy act. But at least I learned how to deal with hearsay when the Judge overrules your objections.

SEÑOR SAL'S TURN IN THE BARREL

A s trial stories go, there is no substitute for a really elaborate criminal scheme put together by a small group of extraordinarily inept and dishonest people. What may start out as a nugget of brilliant criminality eventually disintegrates into a pathetic saga of dimwits stepping all over themselves. This particular tale had its grim turns for sure and it almost secured my pal Señor Sal a return booking at Club Fed. But still. This case was a hoot.

Señor Sal

You may recall Señor Sal from some of my earlier writings. Sal had built a one of a kind legal career which combined flashes of brilliance with recurring episodes of profound lack of judgment. He was smart, creative, and industrious and had developed a booming subspecialty in drug cases, becoming widely known as *El Abogado Drogo*, a street tag he coveted until he started to draw a little too much attention from the DEA and other assorted law enforcement types. As far as the police were concerned, Sal was just a little too creative and industrious since a notable number of his drug clients seemed to walk away with light or no punishment. He fairly quickly got on their to-do list. A bunch of Syracuse cops went to a silk-screening company to knock out a dozen or so *Abogado Drogo* tee shirts with Sal's picture emblazoned across the chest. It was meant to be a warning, but Sal took it as a high compliment and more free publicity.

He was emblematic of the old Amos 'n Andy radio routine where the Kingfish asks Amos, "Hey Amos, how come you got such good judgment?" and Amos responds, "Experience, Kingfish, lots and lots of experience." The Kingfish then asks, "Well, how'd you get all that experience?" and Amos replies, "By havin' bad judgment." Sal had plenty of experience, but it didn't seem to do much to buff up his judgment.

His notoriety brought some financial success and a steady stream of drug clients, but his career was periodically buffeted by one mini-disaster after another. He once had what he thought was a casual and friendly chat with an acquaintance who was a witness in an upcoming hearing for one of Sal's DWI clients facing license revocation. Sal "mentioned" that if the guy didn't show up at the hearing the client (and witness' friend) would probably keep his license. A casual chat. Just sayin.' Imparting this friendly piece of information cost Sal his judgeship in Town Court (in lieu of being charged with witness tampering).

On a darker note, Sal once earned an all-expenses paid but relatively short stay in a Federal prison camp for being just a tad too helpful to a drug client with a wad of cash of sketchy pedigree when the client wanted to buy a modest bungalow for his wife. That caper caused Sal to get his law license suspended for a while, but he bounced back from that episode too, his chest only slightly inflated over his newly acquired rep of "spending time inside." He didn't brag about it; he just saw it as one of the events of his life that made him a macho man. *El Abogado Drogo*.

One of the things that saved Sal was that he was likeable and well liked, and he had a large cohort of friends who were willing to look past his shortcomings. I was one of them.

A Client with a Problem Sal Can't Solve

This particular story starts out with Señor Sal representing a guy named Mr. Burns (an eponymously perfect name for him as you shall learn hereafter) on some kind of Federal marijuana beef. Not a big, big deal, but most people would see a federal drug conviction and some jail time as something more than a minor inconvenience. And in this respect, Mr. Burns was no different than most people. Just a tad stupider.

Young Mr. Burns was one of Sal's steadies, a witless twit who was dependably in recurrent minor trouble. And dependably cash ready. Sal's kind of client. Most lawyers practicing criminal law don't get a lot of repeat business, but as was true in many things (mostly the wrong things), Señor Sal was different. He had a reliable stable of scamsters, scalawags, and cokeheads who provided him with a modest inventory of work and frequent cash retainers consisting of currency of dubious pedigree.

This happened to be Mr. Burns' first visit to FedWorld, a landscape filled with threatening monsters like mandatory minimum sentences for drug offenders and where bail is as common as a Muslim at a Donald Trump rally. Mr. Burns is not happy. He wants this to all go away. Señor Sal can't make this go away. And worse, Señor Sal can't even get him bail.

Federal bail policies and rules being what they are – and, in fairness this really isn't Señor Sal's fault – Mr. Burns activates his self-help button and turns to a bunch of guys who are not only happy to get him out of jail but in fact can get him out of jail: the DEA.

Now, this is not at all uncommon. Given the fact that almost all Federal defendants in drug cases plead guilty and don't go to trial, and that the overwhelming majority of them work the snitch line out to a more lenient sentence by "cooperating" with the Government, Mr. Burns' following this well-worn path wouldn't ordinarily warrant a mention in the morning paper much less a place in this story. And you need to bear in mind that when the Government is looking for "cooperation," they are actually looking for what is called "substantial assistance."

Let me translate that for you. When the Government is looking for "substantial assistance," they're not looking for volunteers to sell War Bonds or help distribute Toys for Tots alongside the National Guard at Christmas time. The "substantial assistance" they're looking for is helping them put the wood to some other yet-unapprehended bad guy, the badder the better, and if it's somebody not previously on their radar (which is more extensive than even the most extreme conspiritorialist can really imagine) that's even better.

I've always told my clients that if you know where Jimmy Hoffa is buried or, better yet, who offed him, you've made it to Substantial Assistance Heaven. Short of that, snitching out another drug dealer is probably gonna save you some time, probably on the back end of your sentence. But still, you're saving time. Would you rather do 60 months instead of 87 if all you've got to do is to put the DEA onto Ramon Up the Street who's been competing with you for years? And, besides, Ramon is an asshole anyway? An alternative consideration, of course, is to be sure that Ramon isn't hooked up with the Mara Salvatrucha or some other murder club; MS-13's got a fat rolodex to work with. And it's not all in Spanish.

So, now Mr. Burns is singing the customary song to the DEA. What makes his show tune a tad unusual is that the audition is being sung in the absence of Señor Sal. What's even more unusual is that the tune is not about that asshole Ramon Up the Street but rather Señor Sal his own very self. We'll get back to the name of that tune in a little while, but let's flash forward a couple of weeks to when Señor Sal thought he was minding his own business at home and I am sitting at my desk waiting for the phone to ring with The Next Big Case. (Sometimes actually happens.)

Sal calls me. The conversation starts out in the usual mode: Sal needs something. For all his trailblazing machismo into sometimes perilous territory, Señor Sal is a very needy guy. On occasion he can show a real talent for many things, frequently self-pity, but this time his affect was an unsettling combination of urgency and mystification.

He tells me he's got this client, Mr. Burns, but the Government wants Sal off the case and won't tell him why except that there is an "irreconcilable conflict." There are plenty of playmates on Mr. Burns 's Indictment, but Sal claims he doesn't know any of these other coconspirators, never even heard of any of them, and he can't imagine what the Government is talking about with this "conflict" talk. Instead of giving Sal a reason, they've brought on a secret sealed Motion that Sal can't see, read, or have and they're asking the Magistrate Judge to remove Sal from the case. I ask him why. He claims he has not a clue.

Earth to Sal: "Burns has snitched you out Sal."

"What?? No. Never! He wouldn't do that to me. Never. Besides, the guy's got nothing to give them."

Long pause. I wait another beat or two. What I'm thinking I should be saying is "Sal, I've got plenty to give them and a) I'm not your client, b) I'm not a criminal, and c) I'm not looking at a mandatory minimum drug sentence."

But I need to help Sal and a condescending lecture – though I'm yearning to give him one – is not going to serve any constructive purpose.

So, for those of you who didn't go to law school, here's the seminar on "conflicts." If, say, you previously represented a witness who is going to testify against your client, you've got something of a conflict of interest. Maybe there's a workaround. Maybe your present client so believes in your devotion to him and his case that he'll say, nah, let's go ahead anyway. And you're able to convince the Judge that your cross-examining the witness who used to be your client won't be betraying any privileges or confidences that once-trusting soul shared with you some time ago, so the Judge says OK, you can go ahead. That's called a waiver.

Here's a harder one: suppose your client finds out that the Government is investigating you. And maybe he's afraid that you're gonna throw him to the wolves to make the Government go a little easier on their case against him. Well, that's a tougher call, but it's also not unheard of for a client to be further emboldened by the thought that you're feelin' the same kind of heat that he's feelin' and he's feeling pretty good about the both of you telling the Government to fuck off. Tougher "waiver" situation, but not impossible.

But there are conflicts and then there are irreconcilable

conflicts and those are not waivable. Where it crosses over from gnarley to no way is when the Government is investigating you and your client is a witness against you. Now, and I'm just sayin' here Sal, you are in No-Way-Jose-Land and the conflict is "irreconcilable." Maybe Sal missed that day in law school. He certainly missed the painfully obvious when he reached out to me for help. Mr. Burns had snitched Sal out and the Government wanted Sal off Mr. Burns 's case.

On the Wrong End of a Court Appearance

Next scene is sort of a pathetic tableau. Sal and I appear in Magistrate Judge Lowe's courtroom only to find Mr. Burns sitting sheepishly at a table, saying nothing, with the standby lawyer who's been asked to stop by just in case Mr. Burns needs another lawyer. Ya think? Neither one of them are exactly a fount of information.

We get even less from the Assistant U.S. Attorney, Carla Freedman, a frighteningly smart woman with a laser focused ability to get her way. For now, her twin beams have targeted Señor Sal and her navigation guidance system is programmed on but one short-term objective: to get his ass off this case. (The short-term objective, of course, is only brunch; the long-term objective is Sal's ass on the menu for dinner). All she's telling the Judge is that there's this "irreconcilable conflict" (she's already spelled it out with details to the Judge behind closed doors), that she either isn't inclined or doesn't have to tell Señor Sal what exactly it is, but that he should be a big enough boy to be able to color in the lines and figure this out for himself.

I get it, the Judge gets it, Carla certainly gets it; only Señor

Sal continues to be mystified. We leave the courtroom, Sal with one client less and me with a commitment from Carla that she'll sit down with me "soon" to explain certain realities.

Certain Realities:
Señor Sal's Life Becomes far less Certain

It takes a couple of weeks, but I finally have a sit-down with Carla.

We are in a narrow and windowless conference room deep in the warren of the U.S. Attorney's Office. There are no pictures on the walls because there is no wall space to be decorated. Instead, I am surrounded on all sides by a series of bookshelves of law reports in impressive binders, each the same book except for the numbers stamped on the red, black, and gold spines. It doesn't matter what the number is on the book's spine; they all say the same thing: We are the Power, your client is Guilty, the only moral thing to do is to Admit Guilt. If you don't believe us, open any one of these books and read what the judges in there say. No one escapes. Give it up.

Carla is accompanied by her supervisor, the Chief of the Criminal Unit, Steve Clymer. If you add his IQ to hers you end up with a nearly incalculable giant number beyond the comprehension of most mortals. Between the two of them they have locked up a modest sized battalion of deviants, drug dealers, murderers, and orcs. But also, between the two of them, they've never once defended a human being charged with a crime. Still, very smart people.

They begin giving me the Reader's Digest version of what

they claim is their case. (Here's another practice tip: when you have these sit-downs with the Feds don't expect more than the Reader's Digest version. It's in their interest to keep you as ill-informed as is legally possible and they are usually operating on the not so unreasonable assumption that your client very well knows what the full story is and it's up to you to choose whose version is the better story when it comes time you're gonna have to retail it to twelve people.)

Their approach is slow and deliberate with just the slightest hint of melancholy over the fate of a hapless colleague who has gone off the rails. They tell it to me with the kind of affect a funeral director has when he has to explain to the family that the crematorium blew up and there's nothing left of their loved one. Except for the part about they're sorry it happened. Which, of course, they're not.

They have yearned for this day, seemingly forever, and now, at long last, they've got the goods. So, tell Sal to give it up, come in, return the law ticket he never really deserved to have in the first place, and, just to make sure he doesn't try one of his patented devious workarounds and try to get his license back, he's gotta serve some serious jail time. Not that ridiculous little time out he served in baby jail some years ago on a tax beef. Serious time. The kind no one really comes back from.

OK. What's the story? Their version: a trio of marijuana dealers (Mr. Burns among them) decided to rip off their supplier by convincing him that the latest bulk shipment to them got intercepted and seized by the police and the truck driver they hired to mule it got popped. So, the weed is gone

None of which is true, of course. The only truth (their

truth) is that they stole the load and then drove over to Sal's house one night and paid him $20K in cash to phony up a police report and a felony complaint about the fictional bust. They then sent the phony paperwork to the supplier to prove the load was gone. So, according to Carla and Steve, my friend Sal is now going to be on the business end of an Indictment and is going to be charged with aiding and abetting a conspiracy to distribute marijuana. I was tempted to add that while they were at it they could also add a charge of aiding and abetting a conspiracy to steal marijuana – but I restrained myself. Neither Carla nor Steve were well known for a sense of humor.

In my line of work, I have a fairly high threshold of tolerance for bullshit. I tend to believe most people, especially clients. And I have heard all manner of experimental versions of reality, from fibs to prevarications, from self-serving deviations from the truth to outright lies.

I'm listening to Carla and Steve and my horseshit detector is fluttering between the Skepticism and I'm-Doubting-This-In-a-Major-Way zones. The only thing preventing me from going over into DefCon1 (Deep Red Impossible) is that Carla and Steve believe it. What I'm listening to from them strikes me as a byzantine tale the foundation of which appears to be USDA certifiable 100% bullshit. But they are not in the bullshit business, as they are happy to remind me, they are in the prosecution business and Señor Sal is going down.

Since I have been polite and behaving myself, they permit me just a few questions. Has Burns pled? Yes. Have the others pled? Yes. Can I see the phony paperwork? Furrowed brow silence. You don't have it, do you? We're working on it.

Ooookaaay. . . Let me see if I can recap this one for us:

You have these three mopes who are convicted drug dealers; they admit not only to a drug distribution conspiracy but to both lying and stealing; Sal helped them lie and steal by producing phony police paperwork; which you don't have. All you have is these three lyin' drug dealers. Am I getting all this right? Sounds like a solid, solid case.

My attempt to bring humor, a little enlightenment, and sharper clarity to the discussion is not appreciated. It has but one effect: we're done for now. Thanks for coming in. You can expect an Indictment soon.

An Unhappy Thanksgiving

The Tuesday before Thanksgiving, I'm in Albany for the semiannual Federal Defender Seminar, a valuable occasion to gather free continuing legal education credits, actually learn something, and generally hang out with colleagues who are dedicated to the cause of what passes for justice in our parts (sometimes it happens). It's also a great opportunity to just shoot the shit with friends.

The crowd is reassembling after lunch in anticipation of the "Views from the Bench" presentation, an annual opportunity to devote an hour or so to hear from a handful of District Court Judges and Magistrates on a variety of issues, not infrequently including coyly couched complaints about how defense attorneys are not doing their jobs properly. It requires absolutely no preparation on their part, merely the ability to pontificate (which they all have in abundant supply). It isn't unusual for each of them to start out with "When I was trying cases . . .," a sure sign that the last case they had as a lawyer was just a year or two after the Code of Hammurabi fell out of favor. Bear in mind also that the most reliable route to the federal bench is graduation from the U.S. Attorney's Office, so basically what is going on for an hour or so is a bunch of defense lawyers being lectured to by post-graduate prosecutors, maybe only 2% of whom actually ever had to defend a human citizen against a criminal charge. But still, it's usually fun if not terribly enlightening.

We are milling about and I find myself in a small clutch of lawyers who are engaged in the main preoccupation which fills the breaks in the program: shooting the shit. Holding forth is Chief Judge Gary Sharpe, a big beefy guy with widely spaced teeth, sausage-like fingers attached to big hands, and, to all appearances to the uninitiated, the affect of a North Country good old boy. Which he sort of is.

Despite a sometimes juvenile and bawdy sense of humor and a proclivity towards practical jokes, however, Gary has a keen intelligence and a compulsion to let you know how smart he is (and, yes, he's a pretty smart guy). When he gets an issue that interests him – or offends him, as the case may be – he doesn't hesitate in drafting a 75 page opinion which not only decides the issue but beats the living shit out of it and then conclusively and definitively refutes even the arguments that neither side has made (Gary showing off that he's smarter than the lawyers who've argued the point). When you get crosswise with Gary and he's on the bench, your life can be pretty uncomfortable. Off the bench, he's a lot of fun.

Gary's telling a joke. I forget what the joke was, but I guarantee you everybody laughed (he's the Chief Judge for Chrissakes). There are about four or five of us and one of our number is Grant Jaquith, the First Assistant U.S. Attorney in the Albany office, a hard charging guy with a well-earned reputation for probity. (Usually prosecutors aren't invited to these defense-only seminars, but Grant was probably there to soak up the judicial brain drippings of the "Views from the Bench" program.)

We're about to turn away from Judge Sharpe when he says, unprompted, out of the blue, "Hey, did you hear that Señor Sal got indicted today?"

Mercifully, Gary hadn't yet been fitted out with one of those lapel microphones for the seminar, but the announcement certainly got the attention of the four or five of us within hearing range. If someone had captured the moment on their iPhone camera, the picture would have memorialized varying degrees of reaction: bemusement and interest in what was a primo piece of lawyer gossip (word had not really circulated of the bubbling stew the U.S. Attorney was cooking up for Sal); real shock and upset (that would be me; no one had told me that Carla and Steve had just gone all in on the story I thought was unprovable bullshit); and, most significantly, ashen-faced horror – that would have been Grant. Grand Jury proceedings are supposed to be secret and even a prosecutor can get indicted for leaking the news that an Indictment has been voted.

Grant Jacquith was really stricken upon witnessing Judge Sharpe's casual announcement of Sal's being indicted. Gary's blurting it out, it so happened, was the result of an earlier phone conversation he had had with Magistrate Judge Dave Peebles who had just received the term's Grand Jury report. Dave had failed to mention that the Indictment had been sealed and he had just signed a warrant for Sal's arrest. None of this was intentional and Gary certainly wouldn't have said anything had he known of the sealing; it was just an irresistible piece of lawyer gossip he was passing on, one judge to another and Gary, being Gary, thought it a choice topic for a casual conversational mention.

Grant was prudent enough not to say anything and proved to be the dutiful soldier he was by swiftly excusing himself from the harmless punishment of sitting through yet another "Views from the Bench" program and heading back to his office. He promptly called Carla and Steve (who were in Syracuse diligently honing and oiling their swords and pikes for the coming battle with Sal and me). They were even more stricken than Grant, not out of any sensitivity over how this news would be received by Sal, but because it upended their careful plan of a blitzkrieg which included the execution of a couple of search warrants (Sal's home, bank accounts, and office) and the placing of handcuffs on the Señor.

Things Get Hurried up in a Hurry

During the next twenty-four hours, everyone's Verizon bill went up. I tried reaching Sal several times. No luck. Carla is furiously dialing the FBI and the DEA to re-coordinate the when, where, and how of the search and arrest warrants. Sal eventually calls me from downtown. The FBI is at his house and they'd like him to come over. Astoundingly, he asks them why and they tell him they'd like to talk to him. Even more astoundingly, he asks me why the Feds are there. Earth to Sal. We've had this conversation before.

It doesn't take long for Sal and me to meet. Except it's not in my office, his office, or his home. Sal is in a locked room at the FBI office and we are informed that they're in the process of getting a Magistrate Judge to conduct an arraignment on Sal's Indictment. For all his prior pretense at mystification, Sal is surprisingly calm. I'm the one who's getting progressively agitated, especially over the ambush quality of how this has all played out. Gee, and I had thought we were all friends.

We don't have much time to chat although there's not a whole lot we need to talk about. Job One is getting Sal released and I'm gratified that Sal's leaving that to me and not engaging in his occasional micromanagement. (But who would blame him for that? He was the one, after all, who's been arrested.)

The door opens and in pops a semi-friendly face. It's Fred Bragg, an FBI agent we've both worked with in the past and someone with whom I've had an especially warm relationship. Fred can be an imposing presence. Being 6' 6" and always speaking in a direct manner with just the right hint of please-don't-bullshit-me, Fred can be counted on to get to the point. Which, disappointingly, he does. I can tell that arresting Sal was not the highlight of Fred's day, much less his career, but, after all the guy's got a job to do.

Almost off-handedly, Fred asks Sal if he's interested in "cooperation," maybe a sprinkling of corrupt judges or D.A.'s or cocaine abusing lawyers we could garnish over the dogshit sandwich the Government has prepared for today's luncheon. . There's just the slightest hint of defensiveness in his asking this, so I'm assuming he's following a protocol imposed by the higher ups (maybe Carla, maybe his Office's SAC).

Since Fred is a direct kind of guy, I tell him he can't possibly be serious. Fred looks down at his feet (which for him is a longer distance than most people have anyway) and says something like "Look, Sal, you've been around. . . . You could really help yourself a lot here." Silence from us. I thanked him for coming by and for the courtesy of not having put Sal in a holding cage. I also added that this conversation's not happening. Expecting that response, he nods and leaves.

Carla pops in. She's leaving town for Thanksgiving and just wants to express her regret (really?) over how things got rushed and tell us were it not for Judge Sharpe's inadvertence we could have handled this more smoothly with a phone call and self-surrender. I tell her how enormously relieved I am to learn all that and I wish her a Happy Thanksgiving.

We then get ushered into Magistrate Judge Dave Peebles' courtroom to get the show on the road. I'm expecting a perfunctory "Not Guilty," we're outta here, and we'll see you in a few weeks. Not. Since Carla was apparently concerned over getting an early start on her Thanksgiving road trip, the arraignment was being covered by Assistant United States Attorney John Katko.

If you needed to have an arrow straighter than Katko you'd have to get a NASA engineer to design one for you. His approach to law, probably also to life, was that the world was divided into The Good and The Bad and if you got rid of The Bad then what was left, by definition and subtraction, had to be Good. This epistemological formula flowed naturally into and supported his corollary theory of criminal prosecution: if you were accused of a crime, you were, by definition, Bad.

Notwithstanding the rigidity of Katko's world view, I always found him to be relatively easy to work with. For one thing, there was never any mistaking where the guy was coming from. For another, what he seemed to lack in compassion was balanced out by his practical sense of what could and could not be achieved at trial. He later got himself elected to Congress where I guess he pretty quickly found out that neither a strong sense of right and wrong nor a talent for the practical are of much use in our Nation's Capital.

Katko announces that the Government wants the Court to set bail. Bail? Both the Judge and I ask the same question at the same time. This guy's a lawyer, has practiced in this Court for 20 years, owns his own home, is charged with a non-violent crime, and knew (sort of) this Indictment was coming. Katko counters that Sal has a previous conviction (yeah, that tax misdemeanor 15 years ago certainly created an ongoing danger to the community) and, besides, he's been drugging and drinking.

Whatever goodwill I was prepared to muster up under all of the circumstances of that day dissipated in an instant and I pretty much popped a cork. The guy's been drugging and drinking? Ya think? The Government's been lurking at his door for weeks darkly growling how they're gonna lock him up and get him disbarred and he's supposed to deal with all that by settling in in front of his fireplace with a warm afghan and a comforting cup of chamomile tea? (In fact I had been worried about Sal's tendency towards self-medication of late, but for the Government to throw this up in a bail argument was simply intolerable to me despite it having a rational basis.)

Judge Peebles decides that Sal surrendering his passport and calling in to the Probation Department every week was a sufficient bail restriction. (Left unsaid, and certainly hovering over all of this like Marley's Ghost, was the fact that it was Dave Peebles who had rather carelessly tipped the news of Sal's Indictment to Gary Sharpe and that, in turn, had led to the Chinese fire drill of the last twenty four hours.)

All that being taken care of, we adjourned to celebrate Thanksgiving, each in our respective ways. Sal was thankful, at least briefly, that he hadn't gotten locked up.

Discovery: "O, brave new world that hast such people in it."

There are two indelicate and enduring truths that every prosecutor eventually learns: "You can't shine shit" and "You don't find swans in a sewer." Notwithstanding these hard realities, some prosecutors still try to make a horse a cow, probably on the not so unreasonable theory that the defendant is a really bad guy, he's almost certainly guilty of something, and they may not get another clear shot at him. I am supposing that ultimately this was the presumed rationale that kept Carla focused on her Sisyphean mission to convict Sal, but as we entered the "discovery" phase of the case, it was pretty clear early on that the case against Sal was wobbly at best.

Rule 16 of the Federal Rules of Criminal Procedure is designed mainly to burnish a patina of fairness over a criminal case. Sort of. The Government has been investigating your client for, oh, two, sometimes three years, sometimes longer, and Rule 16 – in theory – says that they now have to produce most of the evidence against your client so you can "discover" what this is all about. Except when they don't want to. Or don't have to. Or if, say, they have a need to protect their informants or keep secret their sources and methods.

Sometimes it doesn't work out the way Rule 16 intended. After 40 years of this, I'd say that for the most part the Feds are pretty forthcoming (there have been some unhappy exceptions mostly engaged in by truly untrustworthy people, but those are rare). I'll give them this: they are smart enough and cynical enough to know that nobody in the world knows more about the case at hand than your client and in "discovery" all they are really doing is completing the feedback loop that starts and ends with the guy sitting in your office complaining about the fee you are charging and how the Government is fucking him over.

That being said, I was now learning a whole lot more than what I had gleaned from the 20-minute sit-down I had had with Carla some months before. And cynicism aside, I really did believe, at least mostly, that Sal was hearing the full story for the first time too. Sort of.

In its developing iteration, and as made-for-TV plot lines go, it was a pretty good story. One part of it strained at the edges of believability, but other parts had enough of the truth woven through it that a good prosecutor could sell it if they wanted to. And Carla and Steve wanted to. In a major way.

As things came into clearer focus, it turns out that Burns had hooked up with two "associates" in the big box weed business, David LaFontaine and Randy Jareo. The DLF crew as I came to call them, in tribute to the head droid LaFontaine. Were I to compile a list of guys I would least like to meet in a dark alley on a rain-soaked night when I had money in my pocket, tied for first place would be David LaFontaine and Randy Jareo.

Jareo, as I remember him, was a fireplug of a guy with an aggressive demeanor, incapable of smiling except in anticipation of inflicting harm on the nearest person who displeased him. And he was a pussycat compared to LaFontaine.

David LaFontaine was, hands down, the most frightening guy I've ever encountered, in or out of a courtroom. He was a tall Canadian Indian dude whose ancestry seemed to be a blend of Inuit and terminator droid, the kind of guy you'd expect to be astride an oversized Harley alongside Arnold Schwarzenegger. With a lithe and muscular six foot plus frame, he had black close-cropped hair and a pair of deep-set onyx eyeballs which didn't so much look at you as scan the entirety of your body for available portals of entry for disembowelment. It was hard to say who was the "brains" of this operation, but let it suffice to say whichever of this trio of geniuses came up with an idea to do something, it was unlikely that anyone else was likely to disagree with it.

Frightening or not, dimwitted as they may have been, Burns, LaFontaine, and Jareo got caught and now they're all looking at serious jail time. Since they've run out of Ramons Down the Street, their ticket du jour is Sal. I never did find out who exactly thought the Señor Sal part of the plan up, but here's what they knitted together:

The DLF Crew Story

Burns, LaFontaine, and Jareo are buying weed by the multi-kilos from Andre the Canadian, a shirttail relative or acquaintance of LaFontaine. Andre the Canadian, in turn, was buying the product wholesale from a collection of Asian bikers in Ottawa. The bikers are something on the order of extras from a Mad Max movie and nobody fucks with them. Not even the Mafia. But their hydroponic weed is very high quality and there's money to be made all around, so Andre the Canadian is happy to broker their product. He's done it long enough so that the bikers front the loads to him. Not paying these guys back is beyond unthinkable, so Andre the Canadian is super careful about who he ships to and it's the rare customer who Andre trusts well enough to front anything to.

But LaFontaine has earned Andre's trust, so he ships a truckload for further distribution across the border to LaFontaine (as he has done countless times in the past) and the ring of mopes peripherally circling the world of Señor Sal. The weed is supposed to be heading further south into Pennsylvania so LaFontaine and his crew are basically in charge of the transshipment.

So a 50-pound load of Andre's biker weed arrives in Syracuse and sits in a storage shed in LaFontaine's backyard. LaFontaine, Jareo, and Burns spend a considerable period of time staring at the shrink-wrapped kilos in the shed, doing nothing but waiting to be broken down, sold, and distributed. So they can make some money. Yeah, money. Serious money. Enough money to take cousin Louise and her kids to Disney World. Enough money for…. The possibilities seem endless.

And then – and it apparently came as a flash to each of these mopes simultaneously as if the Angel Cannabis had suddenly appeared as a burning bush – how much more money could we have if we burned Andre? Yeah. Fuck him. He's been charging us too much for his product anyway. Let him deal with the bikers. They're all way the fuck up in Canada and not one of them is gonna be making it past Customs at the Peace Bridge any time soon. Let Andre worry about them.

So, like the Old Lodgeskins character in "Little Big Man," they sat down to smoke on it. After rolling a large blunt, they stretched their collective brainpower to the limits (which, despite the contempt I subsequently entertained for these mopes, was, I have to admit, pretty impressive.) Their plan — which they actually executed — was to have one of their number sit in the front seat of a car in Jareo's driveway and call Andre. Which they did. And then — I forget which one of them did this — to deliver unto Andre an excited blow by blow account of how they were at that very moment following the load (right then, right there) along the New York State Thruway when holyshit! You're not gonna fuckin' believe this Andre! the State police pull the truck over! And, Jesus Andre! we're drivin' past this and they got the guy out of the truck and their searchin' it with a fuckin dog!

The two mopes in the back of the car while this driveway conversation is going on are too high to worry about the danger the three of them have just created, and, between deep tokes on the blunt they were sharing, are doing their best to suppress their laughter. They were, of course, maybe 25 miles from the Thruway at this time and the only dog in sight was Jareo's Doberman pinscher taking a pee on a nearby garbage can. Their admiration for this performance knew no bounds (I've gotta believe it was Burns on the phone telling the tale because the two others seemed to me too murderously serious to actually pull this off). They then quickly hang up on Andre, feigning panic, anxiety, and fright, telling him they'll hook up with him as soon as they find out more.

The car is filled with marijuana smoke billowing out one of the rear windows and the three of them roll out of it, hysterical with glee that this actually did just happen, oblivious, and surely not caring, that Andre the Canadian some 200 miles away has just soiled himself with worry about how he's gonna explain all this to the biker crew who supplied the now lost load of 50 pounds of smoke worth over $100,000.

This, of course, was only their planned opening act. It needed a little buffing up.

I've got to give these nitwits credit, they really had thought this through (at least to a point). LaFontaine, Jareo, and Burns could see – even through the cannabis-filled haze of the back seat – that Andre had to have something more than this bullshit phone call (even though they were absolutely convinced that Andre bought the story as thoroughly as if it had just been televised live as breaking news on CNN).

Next stage: let's see. Andre's probably buyin' this story; Burns could have gotten a Grammy for how he delivered it over the phone, but, shit, what if Andre's not buyin' it? It's a lot of weed; if Andre can't convince the bikers that there really was a bust, who knows? Maybe the bikers'll think Andre was in on it and he was ripping them off. No, no, no. we gotta have paperwork. Yeah, fuckin' drug felony paperwork. The kind of shit that gets generated in Court twenty times a day after the cops make a bust. Where can we get fuckin' paperwork? Tick, tick, tick.... yeah, Burns says. I know this guy, El Señor

So, notwithstanding that this is around 9:00 o'clock at night, they decide to pay a visit to El Señor. (To the surprise of virtually no one, Sal worked out of his home.) They decide Burns will do the talking (because, of course, he was all buddy-buddy with Sal anyway) and they also decide to leave Jareo at home. (A visit from both LaFontaine and Jareo at the same time and at night would unquestionably send a person of otherwise normal sensibilities into v-tach.) So confident are they that the Señor can and will supply them with the phony felony paperwork they crave that they thoughtfully bring with them a paper bag containing Krispy Kreme doughnuts, 2 blunts, and $20,000 in $100-dollar bills.

If you've read up to this point in the story, you may have felt a slight titillation and amusement over the scheming gymnastics of this trio of rascally drug dealers. Yeah, it's a pretty funny story. Ripping off the hapless marijuana supplier up in Canada with a phony phone call over a phony drug bust. Poor Andre. Ha, ha, ha. So far.

Now here's the part of the story when darkness starts to descend upon Señor Sal. Not knowing a single thing about the phone call to Andre the Canadian or, in fact, anything much at all about Burns' prior dealings with LaFontaine and Jareo, Sal had no way of knowing if any of this had actually happened. From his point of view, all that did in fact happen was that his sometime client Burns shows up at his doorstep at night in the company of a frightening looking droid and asks Sal if he can take on a case for a friend who just got inconveniently arrested holding a shitload of pot.

This is not an unusual occurrence at El Rancho Sal. At this point in his career, he's pretty much running a DrugsR'Us franchise out of his house providing essential legal support to the recently feloniously aggrieved who may show up or call at the odd hour or two. And because he was good at what he did, recently sprung former clients, such as young Mr. Burns, provided a fairly steady source of referrals. And it was not at all out of the ordinary that Mr. A. was offering to pay the retainer to get Mr. B. out of trouble. Sal had less interest in actually meeting Mr. B. than in receiving Mr. B.'s cash retainer, whether it was supplied by Mr. A., Mr.

B's brother-in-law, or Mrs. B.'s dry cleaner. So apart from the menacing presence of a guy who he didn't know but looked an awful lot like a dark supervillain from a Marvel Comics book, Burns asking Sal if he could represent a "friend" was nothing that the Señor was inclined to find unusual or jot down in his day book of memories.

And, according to Sal, that's what happened. And, according to Sal, that's all that happened. He said yes, Burns asked how much, Sal said twenty grand, and they said OK we'll get back to ya. He gives them a blank retainer agreement form for "Mr. B." to sign and they leave. Name of tune, end of story. Sal goes back to watching Monday Night Football.

Well, not so fast Bunky. There's a different version of what happened in Sal's kitchen on that Monday night: the one being supplied by Burns and LaFontaine. Remember Burns and LaFontaine? The convicted drug dealers? The guys who stole 50 pounds of pot? The guys who lied to Andre? The guys who are now looking at mandatory federal prison sentences for their drug dealing, stealing, and lying? The guys who are looking for help from the Government to avoid serious jail time, the ones who've run out of Ramons Down the Street, so their ticket du jour is Sal? These stalwarts have a different version of the story of what took place in Sal's kitchen.

Here's their story: they tell him what they need. Felony paperwork. Sal goes for it in a heartbeat. Well, maybe not a heartbeat, just long enough to look at the $20K in hundreds, give it a quick count, and agree to phony up whatever paperwork they need.

So, Sal goes down to his computer in the basement, phonies up a felony complaint, police report and maybe docket sheet (plenty of spare ones laying around the Señor Sal archives) and constructs a fanciful tale of a NYS Thruway stop of an Hispanic guy, complete with a trained canine alerting to the mj in the truck (in one version of this story, just for jollies and showing off his artistry, Sal was going to give the dog a name, "Kelly").

He hits Print.

For a quick 20 minutes of work, Señor Sal has earned the cost of a month-long vacation on the Pacific coast of Mexico with pretty senoritas plying him with pina coladas. He brings the papers up to the kitchen where Burns and LaFontaine are in the process of finishing off the Krispy Kremes and one of the blunts. Handshakes all around, hasta luego! and they leave.

Going to Trial: Adventures in Truth Telling

Now, one thing I've learned in practicing criminal law for quite a few years is that "truth" is a relative concept and about the last place you're likely to find it is in a criminal trial, a mini-drama with a host of entertaining figures playing roles of various importance at the conclusion of which you can definitively say that, well, something happened and here's my version. The verdict is just the jury's version.

As the trial became imminent, I went through my usual ritual of sleeplessness at night interspersed with extended periods of worry over cross examining witnesses. My wife is used to these episodes and over the years has become tolerant of my zoning out at what would otherwise be socially inappropriate moments (my kids' school concerts, dinner with friends). She suggested we go out to dinner at one of our favorite local bistros, The Dark Horse Tavern. It's Friday evening and the trial is scheduled for Monday. We happen upon longtime friends John and Barbara Duncan and engage in the usual hihowareya chitchat, in the course of which John mentions he hears that my trial with Sal is coming up on Monday. This particular calendar item was one he was quite aware of, his being at the time the First Assistant United States Attorney and, therefore, Carla's supervisor.

Knowing that John was not inclined then and there to have a substantive discussion of Sal's prospects at trial, I nonetheless can't resist responding with "Yeah, I'm gonna kick Carla's ass." John laughs, I laugh, we both wind up ordering the short rib grilled cheese, a Dark Horse specialty.

I spend a feverish weekend organizing, worrying, outlining what I'm going to say and having my final pretrial meeting with Sal. He is remarkably composed and acts like there's really nothing to worry about. This is either a grand gesture of his supreme confidence in me or, as I then believed, simple delusion. The pioneers at Apple in its earliest phases were both in awe of and deeply resentful of Steve Jobs' habit, inclination, and ability to convince himself of an alternate reality existing in any problem and then bend all circumstances to conform with that alternative. It was called "Steve's reality distortion field." I thought that Sal had a bad case of the same affliction.

But Sal wasn't delusional. He wasn't indifferent to the peril we faced. And he certainly wasn't stupid. Not for the first time in my career, I realized that I had a client who was smarter than me and, despite the incoming shelling, saw our situation more clearly than I did.

The reality which Sal helped to bring me back to was that the Government's case was essentially a re-run of the marijuana smuggling conspiracy that was executed by Burns, Jareo, and LaFontaine and that the story of Sal phonying up documents from his kitchen one night was very much a sideshow. And it was one without any corroboration. So what Sal thought – and this turned out to be the case with 100% accuracy – was that most of the trial time was going to be spent proving a drug conspiracy in which Sal makes, at best, a cameo appearance, exploring the criminal activity of three dishonest and violent mopes; and only then it would turn to a side story about Sal, a story which depended entirely on the jury's willingness to believe these three criminals who were understandably interested in pleasing the Government so that their prison sentences would be reduced.

Still, my job was to worry and if I do say so myself I did an excellent job of it that weekend.

Curtain Up

Monday came and as we entered the leather-bound doors of the courtroom on the top floor of the venerable Pirnie Federal Building, I was reminded once again of how much comfort I took in the dignity of this setting. I enjoyed being in this courtroom more than any other I have visited in my many varied travels along the justice trail. The room exuded a sense of old school dignity and balance, a place where an accused could get a fair hearing in the most traditional sense.

The courtroom was rectangular and quite large, being entirely paneled in walnut and still maintaining the cork tile flooring that was laid down in 1929. The counsel tables were also quite large, accompanied by comfortable leather chairs. The benches of the spectator gallery took up about a quarter of the whole room, all oriented towards the judge's bench, which was also walnut with classical detailing. Despite my love of audiences, I was not disappointed to find that the gallery was essentially empty, save for a single reporter and a gaggle of law student summer interns.

After depositing my files and briefcases, I turned to the Government's counsel table to find, as expected, Carla busily organizing her files and ammo for the day. She was accompanied by her colleague, Assistant United States Attorney Miro Lovric, a nice enough guy who was incapable of saying hello in less than 500 words. I walked over to greet them, and as Miro was nearest I said hello and shook his hand first. I then turned to Carla who, anticipating my approach, stood up, thrust out her hand, and met my handshake with a firm grasp and a mildly ironic twinkle in her eye, saying "I hear that you're gonna kick my ass." I told her that that would be the case (silently reminding myself to be less candid the next time I run into John Duncan).

The trial was before the Hon. David N. Hurd, one of my favorite people, one of my favorite judges. Judge Hurd was that most rare type of Federal District Court Judge, someone who was not a former prosecutor and who was highly independent. As far as the Government was concerned, a little too independent. He was loudly and overtly intolerant of incompetent lawyers (and witnesses) and was mostly known for calling out the Government when they overreached. And as far as he was concerned, that was practically an everyday occurrence. His approach to sentencing was unusual in our District; he allowed virtually anyone who wished to speak on behalf of a defendant to come forward and be heard. He was known to be lenient (the Government thought too lenient) as well as compassionate towards defendants who had been deprived of life's advantages early in their lives, but woe betide those who were privileged swindlers, major drug dealers, or child pornographers. Best of all, he had a terrific sense of humor.

I sensed early on that Judge Hurd didn't think very much of the case against Señor Sal. On the other hand, Carla had a well-earned reputation for competence and integrity with the District Court Judges, so Hurd was certainly going to let her try her case without his interference.

In Federal criminal trials, the judge does most of the questioning of prospective jurors. Some judges, like Judge Hurd, will allow the lawyers limited time to do some of the questioning, but repetition, posing, and wasting time are near hanging offenses so we had to move briskly.

Interestingly, Miro, who did the voir dire (jury questioning for the Government), actually allowed some of the jurors to speak instead of just blabbing at them for 20 minutes; he made reference to the fact that the Government would be calling "certain kinds of witnesses" and no one in the very large courtroom could miss this coded language. When my turn came I resisted the temptation to label these "certain kinds of witnesses" as lying scumbags but the jury clearly got the point. I was pleased when one of the prospective jurors, Mr. Meyers, said he would want to know "why are these guys testifying?" An honest enough inquiry and one which earned Mr. Meyers an early lunch and a trip home for the rest of the week since the Government, of course, got rid of him with one of their peremptory challenges.

Story A, Meet Story B

We spent the morning and early afternoon selecting our jury and by 3:00 o'clock Carla got up to give the Government's opening statement. Before coming to the U.S. Attorney's Office, Carla had been an Assistant District Attorney in Manhattan, a place with real criminals committing real crimes, and she had sharpened her prosecutorial skills over the course of many serious trials. And it showed. She was really masterful. On the other hand, she was well aware of the age-old prosecutorial adage that you can't shine shit. But she did her best. She was candid with the jury in describing her "certain kind of witnesses," to wit: Burns, Jareo, and LaFontaine, as a trio of large scale drug dealers with a history of violence, ripping off other loads of marijuana, sometimes by gunpoint, and sometimes getting ripped off themselves.

She then asked "What's this case really about?" and answered her own rhetorical inquiry by telling the jury that these dangerous miscreants needed someone to "finesse" their latest ripoff scheme by producing paperwork – two pages of altered legal documents in her estimation – that was produced by the defendant, Señor Sal, in exchange for a one time cash payment of $20,000. In turn, the trio of bandidos sent the phony paperwork up to Andre Aubin, their source of supply in Canada, so he could see for himself that the load was lost to the police as a consequence of a highway stop. Señor Sal had made himself a handsome profit of $10,000 a page for his one-time effort.

Not a terribly bad story. Except she left off the part about not being able to produce the supposedly phony paperwork (no matter how many pages it was) and she didn't dwell too long on the reality that her case depended entirely on the three lowlifes she had just derided and castigated for their violence and mischievous ways.

I'm starting to get a little emboldened by thinking a lot more about Sal's theory of the Government's case. It's a heaping stew of steaming gumbo, heavy on marijuana smuggling and marijuana ripoffs, but it only has a dash of Sal. So, as is my preference when I'm giving my opening statement to a jury, I decide to start by telling them a story. Everybody likes stories. Here's the one I told Sal's jury:

Here's a Story:

Guy goes into a hardware store & says to the owner, "I need some trash bags."

Owner says, "I got 5 kinds of trash bags, what kind do you want?"

Guy says, "I'm delivering 50 pounds of MANURE to Utica, I gotta drive it in my car, I don't want it to smell, & I don't want it to break open."

Owner says, "You probably want heavy duty trash bags. How many you want?"

Guy buys just one box of heavy-duty trash bags.

He's now driving down the Thruway & he gets stopped by the police.

One thing leads to another, the police find the trash bags and they are not filled with MANURE they are filled with 50 pounds of MARIJUANA.

The police say to the guy, "You're in a lot of trouble. Where'd you get the marijuana?"

Guy says, "I got it from my friend Andre in Canada."

The police say, "Where'd you get the trash bags?"

The guy is now desperate and sputtering and says, "I got the trash bags from Sal's Hardware Store. Sal told me that if I want to smuggle marijuana, I should use heavy duty trash bags. And he also wanted to sell me a box of moth balls so I could put the moth balls in the bags to cover up the smell of the marijuana. I didn't bother to buy the moth balls. They were too much money"

The police go to Sal's Hardware Store.

Sal's not there.

They look at Sal's receipt book and it shows 25 separate sales of boxes of heavy-duty trash bags that week and they find he routinely sells them.

They also find out that Sal's Hardware Store doesn't sell mothballs and never did.

How's that for a story?

Is that a story about a hardware store guy trying to run his business or is it a story about a hardware store guy helping the driver smuggle marijuana?

Or is it all just a load of horseshit?

I then went on:

As you listen to the story that develops through the testimony of the Government's case, I'll ask you to keep this one in mind. Because all I think the proof is going to show is that two drug dealers come to Sal Piemonte and they ask him if he'll represent a friend of theirs who got arrested with a load of marijuana and when Piemonte gives them a form retainer agreement, something you could print off of the internet, to have the guy sign and come back with the retainer fee, they leave with that set of form papers and nothing else.

He gives them the retainer agreement because that's what he does. He doesn't sell trash bags; he represents people accused of crimes.

They then go and make up a series of lies to their drug supplier and try to make it appear that their fictional "friend" got intercepted by the police with a load of marijuana and they show the guy the retainer form that the lawyer gave them. It's only when they themselves get arrested and are looking at 10 years, 15 years, perhaps life in prison, they come up with a better and more interesting version of the story, one that gets the Government's interest, one that says that the lawyer phonied up a police report to go along with the retainer agreement, a story that they think is going to unlock their prison doors a lot, lot sooner if the Government buys that story. In their beefed-up version of the story, Piemonte didn't just sell them heavy duty trash bags, he threw in a box of moth balls to make the plan happen.

The problem with the Government's case, and I think it's going to be a major problem for you, is that the Government can't show you any trash bags and they certainly aren't going to show you a box of moth balls. What they are going to try and sell you is the word of convicted drug dealers with powerful motives to lie for their own benefit. I don't think that by the end of this case, you'll be in a buying frame of mind for their story. Or stories.

This is a DRUG CASE, but you won't see any drugs.

This is a FALSE DOCUMENT case, but you won't see any false documents

How many lies did they have to tell in order to just get here?

They have a history of lies and betrayal — lies to anyone

and everyone, lies to each other. How can you possibly believe them now?

I could tell that Judge Hurd didn't like my saying "horseshit" in his courtroom, but he let it go because he did like my themes of a drug case without drugs and a false document case without documents (he brought that up more than once during our conferences with the court).

The DEA Crashes on Takeoff

So now the competing stories were set, and the Government gets to go first by calling witnesses. Their leadoff hitter is a DEA agent, John Zaspel, a tall, laconic guy who had worked the case against Burns, Jareo, and LaFontaine and who had collaborated closely with the Canadian Mounties Drug Task Force which had been building a massive case against the bikers up North and their buddy Andre. Zaspel and his colleagues had conducted their own investigation locally, and, with the help of Title III eavesdropping warrants on four separate cell phones, they were all over LaFontaine and his playmates for months, conducting video surveillance, following cars, monitoring deliveries, and learning all there was to know about their operation.

Over the course of the five-month investigation, the DEA agents estimated that LaFontaine's crew was responsible for moving over two tons of marijuana (4,250 pounds) and making a profit of $500-$600 a pound, depending on the quality of the weed. The hydroponic marijuana coming out of the Akwesasne Reservation was higher quality and therefore more profitable. They had such detailed information about this crew that they even knew LaFontaine was fond of paying for his loads by stuffing empty boxes of Tide with hundred-dollar bills. It turns out that the dimensions of a Tide box provide a perfect fit for stacks of hundreds. (You practice law long enough you learn useful information like this.)

Yeah, in response to Carla's questioning, Zaspel was simply overflowing with details and information about this international drug conspiracy and all the players. Except one: Señor Sal. Nary a word about him from this hardworking agent.

I wasn't foolish enough to start in asking Zaspel any questions about Sal anyway. His silence on that subject was good enough for me. The person I was interested in chatting about, however, was Andre, the guy who was LaFontaine's source and the middleman between the Canadian bikers and the Central New York DLF conspiracy using the Tide boxes. The guy who was supposedly fooled by the charade of the Thruway stop that LaFontaine and his buddies cooked up. The guy who they supposedly sent Sal's phonied up paperwork to prove that the bust happened. What about Andre?

Well, I knew an awful lot about Andre by this time. Working the old boy network to lawyers across the border, I found out that Andre and the bikers had themselves been busted. That the Mounties had had their own wire on this crew (tried very hard to get tapes or transcripts of that but came up short). I also knew that at some point Andre had actually visited Syracuse to check on the bona fides of the Thruway bust story (more about that later).

And I also knew that Zaspel had obtained a warrant to arrest Andre should he ever come across the Peace Bridge again. I also knew that the Ontario authorities were not enthusiastic about packaging him up and shipping him down on an extradition request (marijuana offenses were really not that big a deal in Canada at the time). And, finally, I knew that Zaspel had paid Andre a visit up in Canada just to see if Andre wouldn't mind making that short trip down to Syracuse for perhaps a friendly chat with Carla and crew. Andre was not so inclined.

So, armed with all of this foreknowledge I started in by inquiring of Agent Zaspel what it was that he had learned from Andre, particularly concerning the present location of what was alleged to be Sal's phonied up paperwork which, even by this point in the case, had acquired legendary status nearly akin to the Dead Sea Scrolls.

Zaspel wasn't having any of it. My approach to him was as friendly as circumstances would permit and in fact we liked each other. Nonetheless, he just wasn't answering my questions and was giving me a lot of "I'm not sures," and "I'll have to check my reports." A lot of them.

And then BOOM! Seemingly out of nowhere (and to me totally unexpectedly), Judge Hurd loudly interrupted. Very loudly. He started going up one side of Zaspel and down the other, chastising him that when the Government calls agent witnesses in his courtroom he expects them to be fully prepared, to be professional, and to answer all questions put to them. He remarked that Zaspel had no trouble recalling the answers to any of the multitude of questions Carla had put him and that he was not going to tolerate this kind of evasion when a defense attorney started asking questions.

It was a pretty remarkable moment, made more remarkable by the fact that Zaspel was the Government's first witness and this dressing down took place in full view of the jury who, of course, were just starting to size up the Government's case for themselves. Carla was mortified; I did the only thing I could do and should have done, which was to shut up and just stand there. Carla asked for a brief recess so that her witness could review his notes and reports. We broke for 15 minutes.

Zaspel returned to the stand and he was Mr. Informative, confirming pretty much all the things I knew about Andre. Worse for the Government, he conceded that even though he had a warrant for Andre's arrest in his jacket pocket when he went to chat with him, he (and by implication the whole prosecution team) took no steps to even try to extradite Andre. Difficult as it might have been, extradition was still a possibility and they didn't even try. So, I asked him, there were steps the Government could have taken to get Andre in front of this jury to tell us about the phony paperwork, what it looked it, what it said, what happened to it, isn't that right? The answer, if there was one, didn't matter. Just by posing the question, it wasn't difficult to create the impression that the Government didn't want the jury to hear from Andre.

On the whole, this was not a great start for the Government.

The Burns Chronicles

Whatever ground may have been lost in Zaspel's less than stellar appearance needed to be made up quickly and in a major way. That took the form of young Mr. E.J. Burns, the genius of the genesis of the story of Señor Sal and his Magic Paperwork.

Because Carla was (and is) both a professional and a person of integrity, we first had to get a detailed guided tour of Burns' history of criminality. Kudos to Carla for having the jury hear all of this, most certainly in the name of being a prosecutor who was being candid with the jury. Integrity and professionalism aside, this candor with her witness may have had a tiny teeny bit to do with the stone cold certainty that I was going to bring every violent and dishonest detail of Burns' past out in my cross examination, so she was prudent to front load this saga. And there was a lot to tell.

If your idea of a marijuana dealer is a mellow mustachioed stoner wearing a tie-dyed tee shirt in a Cheech and Chong movie and listening to Crosby, Stills, and Nash, fifteen minutes or so listening to the testimony of E.J. Burns would quickly disabuse you of such a notion. He, Lafontaine, and Jareo were ruthless and violent criminals when it came to their marijuana smuggling business, not above wielding guns and using them to betray and steal from others in the same business or those who were supplying their product. This was a real fun trio.

Burns told the jury that he was distributing marijuana on his own for several years until 2006 when he hooked up with LaFontaine and Jareo who together could supply him with 10 to 20 pounds at a time, their sources of supply being LaFontaine's circle of connections in Canada and Jareo's sources on the Akwesasne Indian Reservation. Burns worked his way up into their supply network, first acting as a lookout when cars moving 100 pounds or so would be crossing the border. One time, in early 2007, Burns accompanied a guy named Jeremy Clarke who had 92 pounds of smoke, an "average load," in his car. They were both stopped at the border and Burns, of course, denied knowing Clarke (his first testimonial acknowledgement of a parade of lies in his career as a drug dealer).

They were both detained for a while before being released, the 92 pounds staying behind in Customs' lockup. Distressed over the loss of 92 pounds of product, Burns called LaFontaine to break the bad news and even though LaFontaine recognized that sometimes loads got seized and it was the cost of doing business, LaFontaine wanted proof – paperwork – to show the load got seized. Obviously "paperwork" was one way to show a load was lost and also quite obviously this story got recycled nicely once Señor popped up on their radar some months later.

Burns started moving on up in the DLF crew and within a year he was negotiating a series of deals in a hotel room in East Syracuse with a guy named Damian who had quality product which was being supplied by his partner Todd Crowe, a Native American whom LaFontaine didn't like very much. They were paying Damian in cash, of course, and bringing it to the meetups in trash bags.

Sometime in March 2008, which was the fourth time they dealt with Damian, they negotiated a 45-pound deal and gave him a trash bag chock full of LaFontaine's laundry instead of the green he was expecting. Damian didn't look in the trash bag. But just in case he did, both Burns and Jareo came armed with guns and were wearing bullet proof vests. They eventually sold all 45 pounds of Todd Crowe's weed for $100,000, and for good measure LaFontaine sent Todd Crowe a note telling him to go fuck himself.

A month later, both Burns and LaFontaine decided to rip off a guy named Chuck G. who had a mere 10 pounds. Once again, DLF was motivated by his dislike of Todd Crowe who was the source of this weed, so while Burns looked on,

LaFontaine pistol whipped this Chuck guy. For 10 pounds of marijuana.

Carla then guided Burns' informative narrative of how Señor Sal supplied them with "paperwork" to cover the most recent dishonesty of ripping off Andre as if it was just one more installment of those rascally marijuana dealers just doing what they do, except this time aided and abetted by the greedy El Señor.

According to Burns, the "paperwork cover" (recycled from the border stop with Customs and the loss of 92 pounds) was initially Jareo's idea but Burns' contribution was to call Sal with whom he already had an ongoing relationship. Burns called Sal and told him that he had something he needed to talk to him about. Right away. Could be beneficial to El Señor. Sal complained it would be more "free advice" and Burns assured him that would not be the case.

So Burns and LaFontaine drove over to Sal's house where, in Sal's kitchen, they explained their need for "paperwork" to mask the reality that they had ripped off 50 pounds of Andre's weed. They preferred "police paperwork."

Sal was resistant and unpersuaded until LaFontaine produced the $20,000 in hundred dollar bills that he had thoughtfully brought along (this time not in a Tide box) and, according to Burns, Sal became instantly persuadable, producing through his lawyering skills on his magic laptop "a couple of pages" consisting of a "retainer letter" and a "charging document" recounting the seizure of 40 pounds or more of marijuana. And the lucky lotto winner of these crimes was a guy named "something like" Luis Jiminez.

Sal stapled his business card to these pages and handed them to LaFontaine who, bringing his extensive knowledge of criminal paperwork to bear, carefully reviewed them and pronounced them okey-dokey with him. They left Sal's money on the countertop, four neat stacks of $5,000.00 each, and then left.

Carla then started showing him a series of paper exhibits, all derived from the FBI/DEA search of Sal's home and office. These papers were all from one of Sal's client's files. The client's name was Luis Jimenez. Burns "thought" he recognized some of it, but really wasn't sure. There was a "retainer letter" but it wasn't the same one Burns claimed he saw at Sal's house. There was a Notice of Appearance court document which, suspiciously, bore the date of Burns' and LaFontaine's visit to Sal's house and had Sal's signature on it, but Burns didn't recognize that either. All the rest of the documents were dated around January 22, 2008, at least three months before the Andre ripoff and the alleged visit to Sal's house.

Carla offered most of this paperwork into evidence and Judge Hurd denied her motion to admit the Jiminez file (he admitted the "retainer letter" into evidence but that too was dated January 27, 2008 far earlier than the date that Burns claimed to be in Sal's house). The idea, the suggestion, that Carla was trying to sell to the jury was that when Burns and LaFontaine visited Sal with the plan, Sal already had paperwork for this Luis Jiminez guy "in inventory" and that somehow – the details of this "somehow" never did become terribly clear – that provided a basis to claim it as the template and genesis of the paperwork Burns and LaFontaine got from Sal and which wound up being sent to Andre the Canadian with Sal's card stapled to it.

There were several nasty and inconvenient warts growing

on this story, warts that turned into tumors by the end of the case. For one thing, that Sal would have a client with a Latino surname is as unremarkable as the sun rising in the east. He was not known as *El Abogado Drogo* for no reason. Sal had so many Latin American clients he practically held honorary citizenship in the Dominican Republic. Second, the actual Luis Jiminez was arrested at a carwash with an ounce of crack cocaine stuck down in his pants, a crime noticeably dissimilar from possessing 50 pounds of marijuana on the New York State Thruway. And third, it became more than passingly curious that neither Andre, his biker friends, nor anyone else on the North American continent ever contacted Sal to inquire about the case of Luis Jiminez and the 50 pound load, a circumstance made all the more curious since according to Burns Sal had stapled his business card to the phony paperwork.

Whether the jury was thinking any of these thoughts – I certainly was – while listening to Burns' testimony, Carla then brought us back to Jareo's house where the mini-drama of the phone call to Andre took place. Both Randy and Burns took turns on the phone, in a feigned panic and fright, relaying the witnessing of the Thruway stop that wasn't. Andre could barely breathe between his "OMG's"; almost immediately after the call, he called LaFontaine with a flurry of panicked questions. Why did this happen on the Thruway? The Thruway isn't the route from Canada to Pennsylvania. Why wasn't this on 81? Somehow they convinced him that the driver had suffered a GPS error. They told him that they were going to get the guy a lawyer. Frightened as he was, Andre was insisting that he needed some proof that this had all happened.

I would have paid real money to have heard this conversation. But then it dawned on me that I wouldn't have to spend a dime to get it on CD since, I thought, undoubtedly this tragi-comedy routine was being recorded for later airplay by the Canadian Mounties Drug Task Force, a group of people who had an interest in Andre's every move and moment. Surely, the United States Government, in the person of, perhaps, Assistant United State Attorney Carla Freedman or DEA Special Agent John Zaspel would have a sufficient interest in the wire their Canadian counterparts were running to acquire this 10-minute comedy classic.

Funny thing, though, it never did show up. On the other hand, I had to settle for this small nugget of an intercepted conversation between Andre and Josie LaFontaine (David's sister) on the subject of how well the saga of the phony Thruway stop and Sal's alleged supporting paperwork was playing in theaters up North:

Andre Aubin: Ah, he started to threaten a little bit and I told him, I said, hey listen... He's like, I don't wanna fuckin' hear nothing, I don't want it, the fuckin' paperwork, I want my fuck'n' money. He goes, you better start fuckin' paying starting Monday. I'm like, honestly bra, I'm like, I'm not even gonna fuckin' tell you that I'm gonna give you something Monday. He, I, I'm like 'cause, I'd just be lying. You know?

Josie Lafontaine: Oh yeah.

Andre Aubin: He's like, I (inaudible) fuck, I don't want to hear it. It's been two fuckin' months, you got no fucking paperwork. The fuckin' paper you guys gave me from the lawyer, it was a fuckin' fake. He goes, what do you think I am, a fuckin' dummy? I said listen, I said Evan, you're not a fuckin' dummy. He goes, I've been more than fuckin' patient with you guys. I said, yeah and I appreciate you being patient with me. I said but, I said I'm trying my best to get you your money, I owe fucking three hundred thousand, I said, you know

Andre seemed to be a man in a desperate search for answers. So, he decided to come on down and search for some real ones. It was quite a visit.

Andre Goes to a Softball Game

Andre came, looking for proof, and the DLF crew wanted this visit to be as productive as possible. If perhaps you thought that Burns and his friends were creative with the phone call to Andre, it then probably won't surprise you that they outdid themselves in preparation for Andre's visit. Being a Canadian, Andre was used to watching ice hockey, lacrosse, and perhaps curling, but the all-American pastime of softball was new to him. So, they took him to a Thursday night softball game where Burns was a regular player in a rec league. There they introduced Andre to a team player (in every sense of the word), a guy named Ray Rosario, otherwise known as Poppy.

Poppy was a hard-working law-abiding citizen who liked to play softball on Thursday nights. On most of the rest of the nights of the week, he also liked to occasionally get high on the weed that Burns would sometimes send his way. Although he was aware of LaFontaine and Jareo, he steered clear of them; but he maintained a cordial relationship with Burns who, one night, came to him in deep distress asking for a big, big favor.

Being the team player and get-along guy he was, Poppy

was glad to listen and accommodate, particularly because Burns had confided in him that he was in fear for his life because his Canadian suppliers might be after him over a lost load and Burns needed to explain it. If they could somehow convince the supposedly murderous Canadians that Luis Jiminez was a real guy with real problems and real relatives helping him out, maybe they would spare Burns' life.

So, Poppy being a very quick study, fit right into the requested role of Luis Jiminez' uncle who had posted bail for his nephew after the fictional Thruway bust and was now on the short end of the attorney's fee, the bail, and a lien against his house since nephew Luis was now supposedly in the wind. He was willing to meet and talk with Andre. And – this was the real well-rehearsed shocker – he was gonna claim that he had all the paperwork associated with the case, but he would only give it up to Andre in exchange for $20,000 (a familiar number for sure, one curiously congruent with the number of hundreds Burns and LaFontaine had supposedly slid over to Sal in his kitchen).

As farfetched as this part of the story may sound, this conversation between Andre and Poppy on a North Syracuse rec league ball field actually did take place. Well after Burns left the witness box, Carla put the reluctant and sweating Poppy on the stand to confirm it. You could tell Poppy was telling the truth; he was too miserable to be anything other than truthful about making the greatest mistake of his life by indulging a friend's request for a favor.

Well, it turned out that it wasn't exactly a favor since Burns had reward him with $2,000 in cash for his performance. Not that Carla was anxious to figure out what flavor crime this guy may have committed – remember earlier

I mentioned how smart she was – the story was far too exhausting for average citizens to be offended by one set of criminals defrauding another, so Poppy was never charged with anything and got a walk.

Whether Andre's visit to Central New York made him happy and satisfied (he never gave Poppy the $20,000 requested and that was a good thing because Poppy never had the rest of the paperwork in the first place) or whether his visit was monitored by the FBI, the DEA, the Mounties, or the Daughters of the American Revolution, the one USDA certified, gold-plated, and undeniable fact which came out of this little playlet is that neither Burns nor LaFontaine ever trotted Andre over to Sal's house, never called him, never arranged for a coq au vin dinner, no introductions, nothing. Nada. No contact.

As I listened to the story of Andre's visit evolve from Burns' recitations, I appreciated the significance of the DLF crew never having brought Andre face to face with Sal. They paid Sal $20,000 to phony up paperwork and support their bullshit story and they didn't even try to take Andre over to meet him? Sal's business card was supposedly attached to the paperwork they sent up to Andre. He had to know who Sal was and what his significance to the story of the lost load was. Andre never asked to talk to Sal? Even by telephone? There was something very wrong with that picture and I made it a point to write it out in capital letters in my trial notes so I could bring it up in summation.

To my ever-lasting embarrassment, when it came time for my summation, I got so carried away with the rest of my argument that I completely forgot to mention it. What saved me, I can only suppose, is that this was such a gaping hole and deficiency in their story that at least some of the jurors would ask the question and figure it out. Which they did.

Apparently, Andre's two-week visit to Central New York sufficiently smoothed his ruffled Canadian feathers so that he then accompanied Burns and LaFontaine back to Canada to purchase more marijuana. They didn't bother with the niceties of U.S. Customs & Immigration, deciding to take the trails through the Akwesasne Reservation which straddles both the United States and Canada ("Indians Without Borders" was a familiar tag line). They met up with Jareo who thoughtfully brought along yet another Tide box, this one filled with $60,000 in cash. Despite getting burned (and still totally unaware that his "friends" had fooled him and ripped him off) Andre was happy to be back in business.

Burns then recounted for the jury the events of what was, even for him, his darkest day: August 17, 2008, the day that Carla and the DEA decided that enough was enough and took down the entire DLF crew which included LaFontaine, Jareo, Jareo's wife, Burns, Andre, and practically everyone else who did business with them except for LaFontaine's dry cleaner. (LaFontaine's wife Josie caught a charge up in Canada along with Andre so the DEA left her alone.)

Burns did what most people in such a situation would do (and do do): he cooperated. Sort of. He promptly snitched out Jareo with a nugget of what Burns thought was jackpot information: Jareo, who was already on probation at the time and required to have a full time job, had been paying some guy $2,500 a month for phony pay stubs made out in Jareo's name so he could show his probation officer he was working (these guys really liked phony paperwork). That didn't generate much more than a major yawn from Carla and the

DEA and Burns found himself locked up without bail.

Such a situation, of course, called for the intervention of Señor Sal, and within just a few short weeks Burns sat in a conference room with Carla, Zaspel, and DEA Agent Shane Lavigne (a heavily muscled guy with a great sense of humor which wasn't diminished at all by his daily dose of eating dangerous bandidos for lunch). There too, of course, supplying whatever aid and comfort he could, was El Señor. They sat and chatted for close to three hours but Burns did not seem to be able to come up with anything the Feds didn't already know or convince the Federales it would be a good idea to lift his detention order and get him released on his own recognizance. Sal couldn't make that happen either and the Jareo phony pay stub story wasn't opening any locked doors for Burns either. So, back to Jamesville Penitentiary for Burns.

Funny thing about Jamesville. It's a County lockup but they lease out available cell space to the Feds. (It's actually a real money maker for the County). There's the ample security you might expect for a County prison (housing detainees who couldn't make bail and people convicted of misdemeanors) but it's hardly a SuperMax. Prisoners are able to socialize. And talk. And what a freakin' coincidence, but who else found themselves locked up with Burns? Why it's his onetime pals and coconspirators Jareo and LaFontaine. Jareo is already making a list of things he's going to tell the Feds to get his cooperation deal going. Somehow, the Sal phony paperwork doesn't make that cut and it's not on the list. LaFontaine, unsurprisingly, he ain't saying nothin' to nobody. But, the three of them are talking.

I pressed Burns on cross-examination on the subject of

the three of these geniuses cooking up or embellishing the Señor Sal phony paperwork story while they were all together in the Jamesville lockup and he denied it. I didn't believe him. I'm not sure the jury did either but just asking that question planted the seed of doubt I hoped would grow into a reasonable doubt.

Carla wound up Burns' testimony with his somewhat feeble attempt to explain that he only gave up Sal reluctantly, that Sal had been his lifeline and good to him, and he never really had an intention to snitch Sal out. It came across as hollow and I don't think he earned any bonus points with the jury on the sincerity scoreboard.

In her effort to show the jury how committed Burns had to be to telling "the truth," she reminded him of his plea agreement with the Government which required him to be "truthful and honest." Assuming that Burns was capable of what was for him a high bar of ethical behavior (hard to think of the last time he might have attained it), his reward would be some relief from the drug charge he (and the others) was facing, a charge carrying a mandatory minimum of 10 years in Federal prison. I would say that that was a pretty good incentive to say whatever the Government preferred him to say and, when it came to my summation at trial's end, I said just that.

At the close of every day of every trial in America, the judge reminds the jury to keep an open mind until they receive all the proof. Like many such high-minded principles of the law, this particular admonition bears little relationship to either reality or human behavior. It's simply inevitable that jurors' impressions are being formed as they listen to witnesses and once a sense or perception of one side's story takes hold, it is well-nigh impossible to dislodge it.

By the time Burns left the witness stand after a day and a half of testimony, it is hard to believe, at least in retrospect, that the jury felt much sense of identification or sympathy for Burns and his fellow drug dealing friends and even less of an inclination to do anything which was going to benefit them (like convicting Sal so that they would receive credit for cooperating with the Government and a lesser sentence). Neither Carla nor I, nor in fact anyone, knew this to be so at the time, but looking back on it I would say that the overwhelming criminality and dishonesty of the DLF crew simply militated against believing any more of what was admitted to be habitual lying.

It was about 3:30 in the afternoon when we finished with Burns. I was drained, and hopeful that since it was late June and a very pretty afternoon, Judge Hurd would call it an early day.

Not to be. He sent the jury out for a "mid-afternoon break." Luckily for them, they missed the introduction of our next guest.

The doors parted and trundling in in full prison orange and a complete set of restraining chains came David LaFontaine, closely attended by two United States Marshals of impressive size, dimension, and demeanor.

LaFontaine's Case of Recovered Memory

Manspreading defiantly from the witness chair, still in orange, still wearing leg chains, David LaFontaine was all I could have hoped for. Close-cropped jet-black hair, piercing eyes poised over a flattened nose, his six-foot athletic frame and entire affect projected menace. And for some reason he kept staring at me, as if I was the person who held the keys to unlocking the doors holding him during his mandatory 10-year sentence. Hey, Mister, don't look at me. Answer her questions.

The jury, having been spared LaFontaine's entrance into the courtroom, slowly came filing in, at first curious over the fact that someone was already seated in the witness box, and then silently becoming unsettled when they got a good look at him. We were way past Cheech and Chong movies by now.

With something less than an hour left for the day, I knew I wasn't going to get to cross-examine LaFontaine that afternoon. It would take at least that much time for Carla to de-thuggify him for the jury, trying to humanize the guy before she got to the reason he was there in the first place.

Of course, as far as LaFontaine was concerned, the real reason – and the only reason – he was there was to chisel some time off the 10 year and 3-month sentence which had been imposed on him two years earlier. (Unlike Jareo and Burns, LaFontaine had pleaded guilty pretty early in the case, not bothering to delude either the Government or himself that he would be providing "substantial assistance." Two years in the can, however, brought a change of point of view on this subject.)

Maybe it was a good idea for Carla to get up close and personal with LaFontaine, but not too close and not too personal. He told the jury he was born in British Columbia, grew up in Ottawa, and had never acquired legal status in the United States (although he was in this country often and for long periods of time when he was not in jail). He was 32 years old, had only a 9th grade education, was of Chinese-Native American, Irish descent. He had only met his biological father a few years earlier. He was married (to Jareo's sister Cindy) but was going through a divorce.

Since most of his life was spent as a drug dealer and criminal, we then got a detailed review of both his Canadian rap sheet as well as his current one in the United States. He started out with assault and stealing cars, crimes that earned him 12 months of probation in Canada. He graduated to robbery in 1999 and earned a 15-month prison sentence. (He explained this crime as "wrong place, wrong time," a handy catchall excuse, somewhat similar to "the cops grabbed the marijuana load and here's the paperwork to prove it.") Two years later, he caught a 24-month sentence for attempted burglary, but he only had to do 8 inside. Unresolved and pending in some unspecified place in Canada were charges of dangerous driving and assault upon a police officer.

To the surprise of virtually no one, LaFontaine smoked marijuana every day, but in his opinion it "didn't affect my ability to think" (which, if you think about it, is actually a frightening thought given the crimes this guy committed). He didn't think much of drug rehab programs ("they don't help").

If it can be said that LaFontaine had a skill and occupation, it would be that of a marijuana smuggler. He was introduced to the business by Andre Aubin, a homey he knew "for years," having met Andre in jail back in 1999. LaFontaine was candid enough to confess that the marijuana smuggling and distribution conspiracy that finally jammed up Jareo, Burns, and him was going on well before the Spring of 2008 when the DEA got wind of it.

According to LaFontaine, the basic organizational scheme was that there were Asian gangs in Ottawa growing mass quantities of high quality weed; they provided it to Andre who smuggled it into the United States through the Akwesasne Reservation and then had it driven through Route 37 in Ogedensburg and on to Syracuse where Burns would distribute it, get the proceeds to LaFontaine who then took his cut and send the rest of the money in Tide boxes to Andre back in Ottawa. Jareo had his own connections and sources of supply on Akwesasne and he joined the crew before going to prison in 2004.

That was how it was supposed to work, and it did work. For years. They were generating profits of something on the order of $1,100 a pound, each load ranging from 30 to 120 pounds a trip. And they took a lot of trips.

He recounted for the jury his version of how Burns lost a 90-pound load at the border when Customs seized it and that that little governmental intervention cost them $230,000. Still, as far as LaFontaine was concerned, it was the cost of doing business, since over the long haul only one in thirteen loads got grabbed by the Federales.

He also acknowledged, almost casually, that ripoffs were common amongst competitors, even allies, and he went over the time that he and Burns ripped off Damian, expropriating his 80 pound load (which belonged to Andre and Todd Crowe) in exchange for a suitcase of soiled laundry which Damian thought was $100,000 in cash but didn't bother to look at. (In Burns' version, you might recall, the laundry was in a trash bag.) Just as added insurance to make sure things wouldn't go south, both he and Burns wore bullet proof vests, and each carried a .380 pistol (although Burns' preferred weaponry was a 9mm Glock). Apparently, it didn't raise any alarms or red flags for Damian that these guys showed up at the meet wearing body armor. Such are the ways of drug dealing.

Another time, in the summer of 2008, after the Sal paperwork incident but before they got popped by the DEA, he, Burns, and Bubba Cesario relieved a guy named Germond of $25,000 worth of weed at gunpoint. Although LaFontaine couldn't currently remember the guy's name or whether he pistol whipped him (Burns said he did), he seemed to take some small degree of pride in how well he and Burns worked together. ("Me and E.J. are like two peas in a pod.")

Burns apparently was a gun guy and he supplied a small arsenal of nine guns, including a Mac-10 machine pistol to LaFontaine, but LaFontaine himself rarely carried a weapon. With a face and build like he had, he probably didn't need one.

This brief introduction into the life and times of David LaFontaine concluded that late afternoon's testimony. Although I was looking forward to the next day and his version of the Señor Sal paperwork story, I looked over at the jury. I wasn't so sure they were eager for more.

Judge Hurd had some Court business scheduled in the morning, so we didn't get started until about 1:30. Which was fine with me since I wanted the additional time to go over the multitude of taped phone calls which Carla had supplied to us during discovery. I was looking for one conversation in particular, one which LaFontaine had had with Andre a few months before the trial started when LaFontaine was serving out his sentence at a Federal prison in Mississippi. I found it. It was an interesting conversation.

Whether the jurors had recovered from their discomfort of the day before listening to LaFontaine's criminal resume recital, I know not; but they seemed to be attentive to LaFontaine's retelling of pretty much the same story Burns had told about getting the phonied up paperwork from Señor Sal. Well, it wasn't "pretty much" the same story; it was the *exact same story*, with just a few added details.

No need to go over all of it again for you here, but LaFontaine recalled in detail that the load was 43 pounds; that they got the idea for the phony paperwork when they (Jareo, Burns, and DLF) were in LaFontaine's bedroom; that it was still daylight; that it was in March, 2008; that Randy wanted to use another lawyer; that Burns drove to Sal's which was in an upper class neighborhood; that Sal was in a rush because he had company coming; that by now it was dark; that he was impressed with the granite countertops in Sal's kitchen; that they needed paperwork for an Hispanic male defendant charged with 43 pounds of marijuana on that day's date; that they told Sal that the paperwork was going to be sent to Canada; that Sal went downstairs to print it, saying, specifically, "By the time I get back up here, I want that fucking money on the table"; and that Sal gave them two pages with his business card stapled to it; that he took Sal's handywork, showed it to Randy, put it in a safe, and then sent it on to Andre in Canada.

Pretty good story, isn't it? Just like it actually happened?

Well, since LaFontaine seemed to be such a detail-oriented guy with such a great memory, I asked him about his recent phone call from prison to his long-time trusted friend Andre (who, of course, he had previously betrayed with not only the phony paperwork but the Poppy charade at Burns' softball game). Andre had already served a relatively short prison sentence in Canada but was still on the Feds' want list down in the U.S. I played the whole tape for LaFontaine (and of course the jury). Here are some of the highlights:

Andre AUBIN /David Lafontaine:
January 15, 2011

LAFONTAINE: so what's up player

AUBIN: not much I'm just fucking hanging out. I am going to Best Buy to see if I can get a wireless router......

LAFONTAINE: ok look it, I got something to tell you. I know you already know what happened but I just have to get it off my chest and there is a reason for it. alright there is a reason why I am telling you

AUBIN: alright

LAFONTAINE: I feel bad, you know what I am saying for what I did

AUBIN: ya

LAFONTAINE: you know what I did right

AUBIN: ya its all good, I know

LAFONTAINE: I just want to apologize bro, and why I did it I think it might have been a power thing like having control of like being able to do stuff like that and like no one really being able to do anything about it and shit like that but I just want to apologize to you because like honestly if any body I should have never ever did that to you, Todd that is a different story but you I should have never did it and I should have been honest from the start with you

LAFONTAINE: but all I am saying is like the reason I went back to court was because of the lawyer. I never, listen, I never cooperated my whole case, Andre I swear on my mother's eyes alright

AUBIN: ya I know, I already know that you don't have to explain that I already know that

LAFONTAINE: but look it, the reason why I went back to court is because they trying, EJ and Randi even Cindy they tried to like cooperate against the lawyer and get the lawyer indicted, alright

AUBIN: right

LAFONTAINE: so then check this out, so a month before I got sentenced to the time I got they had me go before a secret grand jury I refused to cooperate I got a contempt charge which

AUBIN: right

LAFONTAINE: which I was suppose to get 18 months extra on my sentence so I thought I was going to get 12 years

LAFONTAINE: now I am in Mississippi and a year later went by and I had my boy go on the computer and I was like yow go see if Sal Piemonte got indicted

AUBIN: ya

LAFONTAINE: he goes online, he has his family go online and he comes back and he's not indicted I am like so I am like yow they need me to indict this fuckin lawyer

AUBIN: ya

LAFONTAINE: so I am thinking fuck it I never cooperated on my case I can live with myself if I fry this fucker.

AUBIN: ya

LAFONTAINE: I am being honest with you Andre alright

AUBIN: ya ya

LAFONTAINE: like I can live with myself, so I am like

fuck it, I wrote, I wrote my lawyer, I wrote my lawyer and I asked her to file for a Rule 35 right, _____ after I get, all the mob guys, see like all the main mob guys that go to trial now, this is what they are doing, okay. Their like, they go to trial, they blow trial and they get like fucking 50 60 years okay _____

AUBIN: right

LAFONTAINE: because all their people are in the court now they have within 12 months to file for a Rule 35. A Rule 35 is that they go back in front of the sentencing judge

AUBIN: ya

LAFONTAINE: their lawyer puts a motion in they go back in front of the sentencing judge and they spill their beans about everything and look it they give an example in this book I read, it's called Busted By the Feds a lawyer wrote it right this one guy had three consecutive life sentences put in for a Rule 35, the information he gave, he got his sentence down to 18 months.

AUBIN: damn

LAFONTAINE: so look it, I put in for a Rule 35 only to fry the lawyer,

AUBIN: right....

LAFONTAINE: so now I am thinking he is going to cop out and if he cops out my lawyer is going to put a motion in and I am going back in front of my sentencing judge and I am going to get a time reduction

AUBIN: right

LAFONTAINE: now my DA also told me this they are like if he, he has to, we have to get a conviction out of him for me to get time off, right, so check this out, if he goes to trial

LAFONTAINE: if he goes to trial and I have to testify against this fuckin guy with EJ, with Randy

AUBIN: ya

LAFONTAINE: with Cindy then I get more time off well guess what I just found out yesterday he is going to trial. They are sending me back to the county they want to ask me some questions well guess what else they did

…..

LAFONTAINE: now one more thing now. I talked to the DA in my case. You know what she told me

AUBIN: what

LAFONTAINE: she's like the only way for Andre to get his warrant off the table is um, all you have, listen to me alright. No one knows nothing about this, your over there I am over here all you have to do to get your warrant taken out is I give you a phone number you call the DA all they want to know is, they just want to ask you questions about what the paperwork that I sent you looked like. that's it. they don't want to know nothing about nothing. all they want to know is about what the paper looked like because this lawyer is going to trial and they want to smoke his boots and

AUBIN: but, but what color, but, I don't remember what the paper looked like.

LAFONTAINE: well, all, all they would want to know is what you remember to the best of your knowledge because me I told them what I remembered and I really didn't remember shit but I just remember that I paid fuckin 20 grand for that shit.

AUBIN: right

LAFONTAINE: I am just trying to figure a way for you to get that warrant off and if you can try to remember anything about it even the name that was on it, if there was an emblem on it

AUBIN: but you know honestly bro

LAFONTAINE: what's that

AUBIN: you, you guys never even gave that to me

LAFONTAINE: oh, it never went to your house

AUBIN: no

LAFONTAINE: Josie said she saw it

AUBIN: that was the fuckin thing from fuckin Todd

LAFONTAINE: what thing

AUBIN: you know when Todd fuckin gave us the paper, remember for saying that he lost the money

LAFONTAINE: oh that paper

AUBIN: ya

LAFONTAINE: that wasn't the 43

AUBIN: no

LAFONTAINE: are you sure

AUBIN: the 43, no that was the 65 that

LAFONTAINE: I remember, I remember

AUBIN: ya

LAFONTAINE: but I know what happened then, we got just like he got it

AUBIN: right but I never had that paper because

LAFONTAINE: you never once even looked at it

AUBIN: I never even got it; you guys never even sent it

LAFONTAINE: no I sent the paper, I sent the lawyer paper I definitely sent it, because he got it, remember you and him were like, you guys were like well, remember you guys were questioning it because it came from EJ's lawyer

…..

LAFONTAINE: I have a minute left on the phone I am going to have to call you back after dinner

AUBIN: so they said they are trying to extradite me

LAFONTAINE: well honestly, if you , if you just, it's like this, I know for a fact that you saw the paper

AUBIN: ok

LAFONTAINE: so if you don't want to do it that's cool but all I am saying if not you have to be careful on the Quebec side if you get caught for anything they can extradite you over here and Ontario they have to pay to extradite you over here.

Phone call ended

In the business of cross-examination, this conversation is known as a target rich environment.

It was hard – if not impossible – for LaFontaine to deny that it was deeply in his interest to have Sal convicted after a trial where LaFontaine fancies himself as the star witness **("then I get more time off . . . they need me to indict this fuckin lawyer")**. Given the guy's fundamental deviousness and dishonesty, it was not hard to imagine that he would say virtually anything to benefit himself, especially when his liberty was at stake. **("I can live with myself if I fry this fucker")**

He tells Andre about the wonders of Rule 35 of the Federal Rules Criminal Procedure (where the Government can ask for leniency after a sentence has already been imposed) as if he was a W.W. II scientist telling a colleague about the discovery of penicillin **("this one guy had three**

consecutive life sentences put in for a Rule 35, the information he gave, he got his sentence down to 18 months" . . . **"I put in for a Rule 35 only to fry the lawyer."**)

Uncomfortably for Carla (and, to a lesser degree, me), LaFontaine seems to be if not married to Carla at least in her thrall and employ and they are working together to achieve a mutually desired goal. **("now my DA also told me . . . , we have to get a conviction out of him for me to get time off")** In other recorded jail conversations (I was supplied with about seven hours' worth of them), Lafontaine can be heard recounting all of the things Carla and the Government team would be doing for him: better placement in county holding facilities, the dropping of a warrant for his sister Josie, assistance with obtaining a visa to re-enter the country (he is a Canadian), and the voluntary surrender without penalty of machine guns and vests which were not originally seized by the authorities. The gist of these phone calls, suggesting that Carla was practically buying La Fontaine's testimony (from his point of view) was sufficiently disturbing to me that prior to trial I wrote a letter to Steve Clymer, the Chief of the Criminal Bureau in the U.S. Attorney's Office suggesting that Carla step off of the case, not because she was doing anything inappropriate or unethical (an absurd suggestion) but rather that she could become an unsworn witness in the trial. Steve wrote back with a thoughtful response politely telling me to kiss off. (I never pursued it).

In this phone call with Andre, Lafontaine even more deviously tries to persuade Andre that it would be in his (Andre's) interest to cooperate with Carla and the prosecution team and help them out (**"she's like the only way for Andre** to get his warrant off the table is um, all you have, listen to me alright. No one knows nothing about this, your over there I am over here all you have to do to get your warrant taken out is I give you a phone number you call the DA all they want to know is, they just want to ask you questions about what the paperwork that I sent you looked like. that's it. they don't want to know nothing about nothing. all they want to know is about what the paper looked like because this lawyer is going to trial and they want to smoke his boots")

Apart from the fact that I became enamored of the expression "smoke his boots" (I had never heard that turn of phrase before and I made a mental note to thank LaFontaine for the vocabulary enhancement), what really interested me was that part of the conversation where the two of them are dancing around "the paperwork," a subject which, of course, was at the very heart of the case against Sal. In what was nearly a comical minuet of false denial between the two them, Andre is telling LaFontaine he never got the paperwork in the first place and LaFontaine is trying his best to convince Andre that yes you did:

AUBIN: but, but what color, but, I don't remember what the paper looked like.

AUBIN: right but I never had that paper because

AUBIN: I never even got it; you guys never even sent it

AUBIN: you, you guys never even gave that to me

LAFONTAINE: no I sent the paper, I sent the lawyer paper, I definitely sent it, because he got it, remember you and him were like, you guys were like well, remember you guys were questioning it because it came from EJ's lawyer

LAFONTAINE: well honestly, if you, if you just, it's like

this, I know for a fact that you saw the paper

I'm not sure where all of this left the jury, but it surely couldn't have been anyplace good for the Government.

For me, the jackpot and payoff for the entire conversation was Lafontaine saying **"because me I told them what I remembered and I really didn't remember shit but I just remember that I paid fuckin 20 grand for that shit."**

Now, there was a statement I could believe in and more than live with. Whether he was in his customary marijuana haze when he was at Sal's house, whether the incident was just one in a long line of phony paperwork ripoff schemes, whether it was so long ago he really couldn't remember if he tried, or (my preference) he forgot what version would be most helpful to him, the truth – if there was a truth – was such a far distant concept for LaFontaine he wouldn't know it if it came up to him on the witness stand and kissed him. Remember how he told the jury how much he admired Sal's granite kitchen countertops? Here's a pop quiz: you think that that was an accurately recovered memory of his actually being there or the function of his being prepped for trial by Carla and Miro who showed him the DEA videotape of Sal's house when they executed the search? Which do you think is the more likely source?

I confronted LaFontaine with the tape and his statements of how the Government was going to help him, that if Carla convicted Sal and smoked his boots it would be good for him, and how he tried to convince Andre to cooperate with the Government and suddenly remember that, oh yeah, he did get that paperwork. Carla, of course, was expecting this kind of cross examination and she would not have been doing her job if she had not prepared LaFontaine accordingly to have at least some response.

The best that LaFontaine could do was to say that he knew the calls were being recorded, that he was only trying to bait Andre, and that he was just plain "confused" about Rule 35 and what the Government could do or was willing to do.

I concluded my cross of David LaFontaine by asking a question which was exclusively for the jury's benefit; LaFontaine's answer was completely immaterial and irrelevant. It was just a thought that I wanted to leave the jury with: *"Do you agree that the only way we can know what Andre really thought or meant about Poppy, the paperwork, the rips, or anything else is to have him in here to testify and let this jury decide what the truth is?"* Carla objected, too late. LaFontaine said yes.

Compliments of Agent Zaspel, I knew that Andre was never going to show up.

The Parade of Witnesses
Who Never Met Señor Sal

It wasn't really all over but the shooting with the appearances of Burns and LaFontaine, but the rest of the Government's case consisted in the main of testimony from people who either never met El Señor or had little or nothing to do with him.

We heard from David LaFontaine's sister Josie, a particularly sad witness who had led a particularly sad life of single motherhood, drug addiction, prostitution, bipolar illness, arrests, deportations, and rehabs. She was just inside the periphery of the drug business run by her brother and knew and dealt with the whole crew at various times (Andre, Damian, Randy, Burns, Todd Crowe). She never met Sal.

Josie LaFontaine didn't move the Government's case

forward so much as attempt to reinforce that same story the jury had already been told: the ripoff of Andre's load, the paperwork (which she claimed to have seen), Andre's visit. Her only contribution to the case against Sal was that she remembered seeing a business card with the paperwork with the name "Salvatore" on it. (Remember that Burns was one of Sal's steadies and his having Sal's card in his wallet would be as unremarkable as his having a driver's license in there.)

Presumably on the assumption that Carla believed in The Rule of Three, the principle that suggests that a trio of events or characters is more satisfying or effective than other numbers, Randy Jareo then took the stand to educate us all on his career in criminality and the marijuana smuggling business with LaFontaine and Burns. Jareo had been to many places (Akwesasne, Ottawa, Syracuse, jail) but missing from his TripAdvisor itinerary folder was Sal's kitchen. He had never met the good Señor but was ready to fill us all in on the interstices of the story his coconspirators had previously detailed for us.

Jareo had been continuously in jail since his arrest three years earlier. He had pleaded guilty to the marijuana conspiracy two years ago, but he had not yet been sentenced. After signing a plea agreement with the Government, he was hoping for some leniency and wiggle room from the mandatory minimum of 10 years he was facing. Marijuana smuggling was his thing, although at one time he tried his hand at cigarette smuggling as well. Given his track record, neither occupation was a good fit for him. He caught a 5 year sentence in Canada for tax evasion, marijuana cultivation, and cigarette smuggling sometime in the 1990's.

Moving his act south, he was convicted of felony

marijuana possession in 1996, and then he stepped it up big time in 2005 when he pleaded guilty in Federal Court to moving 100 kilos of marijuana. When Jareo was sentenced by U.S. District Court Judge Frederick J. Scullin, Jr. to a sentence of 28 months and 4 years of supervised release, he told Judge Scullin "you'll never hear my name again." It was only 2 years later that Judge Scullin heard Jareo's name again.

While on his supervised release (federal parole), he was working odd and sporadic jobs, some real some fictional (he paid for pay stubs "Just to keep Probation happy"), he hooked up again with LaFontaine, who he met in prison in 2001, in moving marijuana across from the Akwesasne and the Canadian border.

A note about the Akwesasne Indian Reservation and "the Canadian border": Akwesasne is an ancient and sovereign Indian territory and it extends well into both New York State and the provinces of Canada. Like many Native American enclaves, it has a host of social problems, alcoholism, drug addiction, and poverty among them. A major occupation on the Rez is smuggling; it is a way of life. Culturally, and every other way, the Natives of the Akwesasne just don't recognize or accept that moving goods across the St. Lawrence River, from one side of the Rez to the other, is "smuggling." When Natives are charged in U.S. courts with smuggling either into or out of Canada, the common refrain is "Where the fuck is Canada?"

Jareo gave the jury yet another series of rip stories, stealing from colleagues and competitors apparently being an integral part of the marijuana smuggling business. LaFontaine was constantly complaining that he was getting ripped off, so it was nothing out of the ordinary when Jareo participated in the Damian dirty laundry in a suitcase caper. Jareo drove, so he got $20,000 for his part of the $100,000 booty. When LaFontaine and Burns took a trip to California in May 2008, Jareo occupied his time by helping Adam Bigtree rip off a 100-pound load of weed.

Jareo seemed to be disappointed that he never met Sal. He had his own lawyer in mind for the phony paperwork setup but then had second thoughts on that subject and settled for Sal when Burns recommended him.

His main testimonial contribution to the trial seemed to be that he remembered seeing the "2 pieces of paper" that LaFontaine and Burns came back with. One was a retainer letter with a Spanish name and the other referred to marijuana, the make of a car, and that Spanish name again. LaFontaine told him that he had to pay $40,000 to Sal. Jareo's version of this reality had the phone call to Andre occurring a day or two after the paperwork was commissioned, but I don't think that made much difference. He described the frantic phone call to Andre as "all lies," a common language that the entire crew shared and was comfortable with.

To prove to the jury what a standup guy he was, he said that he told the DEA "from the get-go" (the day of his arrest in August 2008) that he was ready to cooperate. Apparently, even mentioning the phony paperwork story didn't come about until two months later. And Jareo was sure that he had had no contact or conversation of any kind with either LaFontaine or Burns since they were all arrested (despite the fact that all three shared guest quarters in Jamesville Penitentiary for about six months).

From Jareo's testimony, and from Josie's earlier, the jury could conclude that the paperwork with the Spanish surname and the retainer letter could possibly be what LaFontaine and Burns claimed they paid Sal $20,000 for: a set of fraudulent documents customized to give support to their theft of Andre's 43 pounds of marijuana. On the other hand, given the fact that this story is emanating entirely from the mouths of liars, criminals, and thieves who spent more time high than the average person spends breathing, the paperwork could also possibly be what Sal claimed it was: a sample retainer for Mr. B when Mr. A was going to pay for the representation.

Of course, Andre could have enlightened everybody on what the paperwork actually said and consisted of, but after his taped jail phone call with LaFontaine it would be hard to imagine the degree of credibility the jury would have accorded him. And besides, Andre seemed to be on a permanent camping trip with the Himalayan Yeti, so we never did hear from him. Trash bags and moth balls; it depends on your point of view.

What doesn't depend on your point of view is this: "could possibly be" doesn't feed the bulldog. We are dealing with a criminal case, a serious one. "Could possibly be" is not the standard. The standard is "proof beyond a reasonable doubt" and we were as far away from that as we were from Andre's front porch.

The remainder of the Government's case was essentially devoted to housekeeping matters. Supervising DEA Agent Tony Hart (a very professional guy who maintained his sense of equanimity under all circumstances that I know of, although truth to tell he never raided my home or office at gunpoint) told the jury how he led the team of 8 agents who conducted the 3 hour search of Sal's home and office (it was the same place). He narrated the video tour of the house (with outstanding views of Sal's granite countertops) and identified a client file they seized ("Luis Jiminez," by now a familiar name to the jury). He also identified the two computers, one laptop, one desktop, seized from the first floor.

Tony Hart was followed by his DEA colleague Ken Haynes who was a Digital Evidence Specialist. He examined both the laptop and the desktop and found numerous documents relating to Luis Jiminez (which wasn't a shock to any of us since even Carla conceded that Luis Jiminez was a real person, a real client of Sal's, and was burdened by a real crack cocaine case against him). What was interesting, however, is that only the desktop in the basement had Luis Jiminez files on its hard drive; there weren't any on the laptop. I don't know how many jurors thought to recall that Burns was pretty clear on Sal composing whatever he composed *on his laptop* right there on the granite countertop, but I made a note to remind them.

The Government wrapped up their case against Sal by calling representatives from two banks where Sal conducted his business. Solvay Bank had a record of a cash deposit of $5,000 in September 2007 (8 months before LaFontaine and Burns' visit) and Citizens Bank sold Sal a $20,000 Certificate of Deposit in October 2008 (5 months after LaFontaine and Burns' visit). I'm not sure what this was supposed to have proven, especially because it would be unlikely in the extreme that if Sal was dealing in drug money cash, especially $20,000 fresh out of a Tide box, he would have put the money in a bank.

Thus ended the Government's case in chief against Señor Sal.

Our Turn

I have previously written that if you stand in front of a jury in your opening statement and remind them that the burden of proof is always on the prosecutor and you and your client don't have to prove anything at all, you would then appear to be either a moron or a hypocrite if you go on to tell them what you're going to prove. That was especially so in Sal's case because, in fact, we had nothing to "prove." Our defense consisted of challenging the prosecution's proof and witnesses so vigorously that no reasonable person could do anything other than conclude that they had a reasonable doubt as to Sal's guilt. That was the defense. The Government had no case.

But still, I felt (and Sal agreed) that there was at least one point we'd like the jury to consider that wasn't worked into the Government's case and it was something we thought was relevant and important: Sal's computer skills were near hopeless and he was heavily dependent on his devoted secretary Sheila Collins to compose everything from envelopes with addresses on them to briefs to be submitted to the Appellate Division. It's not that Sal couldn't spell, but even the simplest keyboard tasks were quite beyond him. Since there was never a thought to having Sal take the stand in our case, we still thought that there should be some counter to both LaFontaine and Burns describing the ease and promptness with which Sal "knocked off" the requested tricked up paperwork. Our short answer: Sal couldn't do this.

Sheila took the stand and said what was to be said on the subject of Sal's rudimentary computer skills. She also kept fairly careful track of his finances, particularly noting that in

September 2008 Sal got a property damage settlement check from State Farm insurance in the amount of $16,000. I brought this up just in case any of the jurors were suspicious of the $20,000 CD purchased from Citizens Bank a month later, in October 2008.

Carla didn't do much with Sheila, although I do think she stooped rather low in challenging her on a check register Sheila maintained which was in blue ink, black ink, and pencil. Apparently, Carla never tried running her own office.

Closing It Down

It was time for summations. One of the realities I have come to accept after 40 years of doing criminal trial work is that no matter how hard and meticulously you prepare your summation, it really doesn't count for very much or make a significant difference. No trial lawyer wants to either admit or accept the fact that the jury has made up its mind long before you are choosing what suit to wear on the morning of the close of the trial. The opening statement is far more important and if the jury isn't with you by mid-trial, a great summation won't save your cause. It'll just be entertainment.

To be candid, I don't remember a single thing about the two summations the Government gave. Yes, they get two. They open and then they have the last word after you've left your heart and tears on the courtroom floor. Not terribly fair in my view, but da rules iz da rules.

The trial lawyers amongst you will recognize the truth of this, but the fact of the matter is that I had been summing up all trial. A lot of the questions I posed to witnesses during the trial weren't really intended to be answered. What they were were post-it notes to the jury to think about this subject or that idea.

I suppose I was somewhat operatic, perhaps pontificating, perhaps emotional (after all, Sal was my long-time friend) in my summation. I can't recall. But here in an abbreviated format is what I said to the jury:

Guy goes into a hardware store ....Oh, that's right, I told you that story already.

Is that what happened here?

Burns & Lafontaine ask Piemonte to represent one of their couriers, he gives them a retainer agreement & they leave. Is that consistent with the proof in this case? Or has the Government proven something darker?

These people aren't just drug dealers. They are dangerous drug dealers. Even worse than that, they are dishonest drug dealers. They will lie and betray and look for any advantage to "get over" on someone else if they think it's going to benefit them. And don't for a minute think that they are not looking to benefit themselves. What is more precious to anyone other than their own freedom? What would you do or say to avoid spending 10 years in jail?

Can you really look past their moral failings? their legal failings? their character failings? & say "yes, I can take their word for it this time. They're telling the truth. I'm convinced beyond a reasonable doubt of what they have to say here"? Can you? Should you? Would you base a serious decision about an important matter in your own life or that of a loved one on the dependability of any one of these people? That's really the question here. Do you know why? Because that's all there is to the Government's case. Their word.

Would you make a serious decision about a matter which

was important to you and your family based upon the word of any one of them? All of them? In my opinion, No reasonable person would.

PAPERWORK? – WHAT PAPERWORK?

Where's the RETAINER LETTER?

Where's the NEW YORK STATE POLICE SEIZURE FORM?

WHERE'S ANY DOCUMENT SHOWING THAT 43 POUNDS OF MARIJUANA GOT TAKEN ON A SPECIFIC DATE?

Even if such paperwork existed – ever – how can you say it came from Sal Piemonte?

There is no file on his laptop – and Burns says Sal printed it off of his laptop.

And where is ANDRE? If the Government thought you ought to hear from Andre, they could have at least taken steps to try and get him here. But they didn't.

I tend to get carried away with the sound of my own voice and the drama of my own rhetoric. On the whole, I thought that my summation in full was pretty good. Of course, nobody's perfect and I remember – clearly – writing out in my trial notes in BIG CAPITAL LETTERS that it was worthy of comment in my summation that when Andre came down for his two week visit nobody brought him to talk to Sal. It was – or would have been – not only a brilliant observation but a brilliant argument. Brilliant. But I got so carried away by my own rhetoric that I simply forgot to address or even mention it. Brilliant. In fact, while we were waiting for the jury, Judge Hurd complimented me on my summation, but also added "Hey Eddie, you left out the part about their never introducing Andre to Sal. I thought that was your best argument." Brilliant.

I Get to Go Back to My Office

There's an old New York City trial lawyer story, probably apocryphal, about a guy named Sam Liebowitz who had the longest string of death penalty acquittals in Manhattan history. It was pure magic. You wanted to stay alive and be found Not Guilty, you hired Sam Liebowitz. One day, as it inevitably would come, his client is convicted and is now facing death. As the jury was filing out, the client turns to him and says "So, what do we do now Sam?" and Liebowitz replies "Well, I don't know about you, but I'm going back to my office."

Cynical as that story is, it has an enduring truth at its heart. I live and die with my clients and brave the hurly-burly with them, suffering the needles of the wind and the buffeting of the lance. I share in their elation and relief when they are acquitted, and I feel the depth of their devastation when they are convicted. But, still, like Sam Liebowitz, at the very end of it all, I get to go back to my office.

Waiting for a jury is one of the worst experiences in life. It is like being an expectant father and being barred from the delivery room. Every creak of the swinging door, every movement of a functionary, raises your anxiety. A jury sends out a note asking a question or requesting an exhibit and lawyers pour over it like it was a Rosetta stone bearing a message nearly impossible to decode or decipher. Lawyers are control freaks. I'm probably one, although I honestly think I can control that impulse to an acceptable degree. But with a jury out, and you being able throughout the whole trial to influence and control how things go, it is utterly maddening to have no ability to dictate what's going on or what's being talked about. You just have to wait.

After Judge Hurd gave them their final instructions, the jury retired to deliberate at 10:25 a.m. They talked, ate lunch, talked some more, and about 3½ hours after they started, they reached a unanimous verdict. There is a terrible swiftness to a jury verdict; the longer the trial, the stranger it seems that there is such a sudden resolution that you have worked so hard for and desired so much. It is a frightening moment because so much is at stake. A person's fate is pronounced in less than 30 seconds and it is terrible.

Because of the size of the courtroom, Sal and I sat at a table far distant from the jury box and Sal, who was deaf in one ear, had trouble hearing "Not Guilty." I had to repeat it to him. He shuddered slightly and then leaned his head on my shoulder. We gathered our stuff, I went over to shake Carla's hand and Miro's, and then we left the courthouse. It was a warm and beautiful day.

Epilogue

Three months after the trial, David LaFontaine got his wish for Rule 35 relief and his previous sentence of 123 months was reduced to 57 months. He served another year and was released in October 2012.

Randy Jareo was facing a mandatory minimum sentence of 120 months. In consideration of his testifying, the Government moved to reduce his sentencing range and he was sentenced to 46 months. He was released in May 2012.

E.J. Burns was sentenced to "time served" (6 months) and got probation.

Sal Piemonte returned to practicing law, but he never

really recovered from the experience of the trial. As of this writing, his license has been suspended once again.

I went back to my office.

ABOUT THE AUTHOR

Ed Menkin is a criminal defense lawyer in Syracuse, New York. A proud son of the Bronx with a Ph.D. in Shakespeare, he has hiked across the Grand Canyon and ridden a hot air balloon over the Serengeti Plains at dawn. But his greatest adventures, and his most fun, have taken place in Court and these are some of his stories.

For more information about Ed, please visit his website:

www.edmenkin.com

Made in the USA
Middletown, DE
26 August 2019